THE MORALITY OF SELF-INTEREST

Robert G. Olson

AN ORIGINAL HARBINGER BOOK

HARCOURT, BRACE & WORLD, INC.
New York · Chicago · Burlingame

TO JUSTUS BUCHLER

Library of Congress Catalog Card Number: 65–18123

PRINTED IN THE UNITED STATES OF AMERICA

PREFACE

The Morality of Self-Interest deals with most of the problems traditionally discussed by moral philosophers—reason and ethics, egoism and altruism, conscience, freedom and determinism, the development of moral character, ethics and religion, etc.—but from a distinctive point of view. The principal contentions are that questions of personal ethics cannot, as is all too commonly thought, be divorced from questions of social policy; that an act cannot be considered right unless it promotes the well-being of both the agent and society; that the individual is most likely to contribute to social betterment by *rationally* pursuing his own best long-range interests; that rational procedures of the kind employed in the empirical sciences are in principle competent to define moral terms and determine the truth or falsehood of moral judgments; and that prevailing religious views, far from being conducive to moral uprightness, in fact seriously undermine the practice of morality.

This book is addressed not only to professional philosophers, but also to scholars in other fields, especially the behavioral sciences, and to the intelligent general reader. Technical terms, therefore, have been used sparingly and defined when introduced, references to philosophers have been kept to a minimum, and where it has been deemed necessary to criticize another thinker his position has first been expounded. At no point, however, have I simplified the statement of my position or omitted essential arguments in order to attract more readers.

Many persons will be disturbed by a number of psychological and sociological generalizations offered in this work that are inadequately supported by statistical data or controlled experimental investigation. In this connection I should like to make two points. First, Aristotle's dictum that the wise man will not demand greater certainty than the subject matter allows still holds good. All of us do constantly make practical moral decisions that presuppose beliefs with respect to human psychology and the probable social consequences of our behavior. Although it would be infinitely desirable that these beliefs all be of the kind that psychologists and social scientists could certify as true or false, the simple fact is that most of them do not as yet fall into this category. And where this is the case, a philosopher can only make these beliefs explicit, approving or rejecting them on the basis of whatever evidence is presently available, allowing such things as consistency with other, better-confirmed beliefs and the testimony of common sense to count as evidence. Imperfect though criteria of this latter kind are, they are better than none at all, and the alternative to invoking them is to abandon altogether the practice of moral philosophy as traditionally conceived. Second, it is my hope that this book will come to the attention of behavioral scientists and encourage them to make the experiments needed to validate or invalidate any generalizations they regard as questionable. If this hope is borne out, *The Morality of Self-Interest* will have served a useful purpose even if every contention in it is proved false.

One last word. The issues under investigation are complexly interrelated. For the sake of clarity in exposition, I have attempted to break them down into relatively independent problems corresponding to the chapter titles and the subheadings within the chapters. None the less, the reader is asked to regard this book as a single continuous argument. Most chapters elaborate upon and give further support to positions taken in previous ones. I wish to insist upon this, since many points made in an earlier chapter will inevitably raise questions in the reader's mind, to which a satisfactory answer is forthcoming only at a later stage in the argument. Several points in Chapter 1 may even strike the reader as wildly paradoxical, but subsequent elaboration and defense will, I believe, do much to dispel this initial impression.

ROBERT G. OLSON

ACKNOWLEDGMENTS

I am grateful to the following persons, who read an earlier draft of this study and made many helpful suggestions: Raziel Abelson, William Alston, Gail Belaief, Justus Buchler, William Frankena, Fred Goldin, the late Paul Henle, Mary Mothershill, and Stephen W. Rousseas. As is customary, I should like to absolve these persons of any responsibility for errors and inadequacies. It is especially important that I do so, since their views on ethics often differ sharply from my own and I often stubbornly refused to follow their suggestions.

A special debt of gratitude is due Justus Buchler, with whom I have had the good fortune of associating as a colleague from 1958 to 1961 and in the last few years as a fellow member of the Philosophical Group of New York. Although my own work differs substantially in both content and style from that of Professor Buchler, I hope it reflects the same fidelity to the seriousness of the philosophical enterprise. In any event, *The Moralty of Self-Interest* would be a very different book were it not for his influence. My over-all philosophical orientation has been shaped to a great extent by lectures he delivered when I was a graduate student at Columbia University and by his published work, especially his *Toward a General Theory of Human Judgment.* Moreover, he has helped me give birth to many ideas that would otherwise not have seen the light of day. Great philosophers and great teachers are both rare, but the combination is even rarer, and it is a privilege to be able to testify to the reality of that combination in the person of Professor Buchler.

CONTENTS

chapter one

PERSONAL WELL-BEING AND SOCIAL WELFARE

The most crucial problems in moral philosophy have to do with real or alleged conflicts between the interests of the individual and the interests of social groups. Unfortunately, the layman who picks up a book of moral philosophy in the hopes of finding a solution to these problems is likely to be disappointed. The solutions proposed by traditional moral philosophers, who did give these problems the attention they deserve, have lost much of their cogency. Most contemporary moral philosophers, on the other hand, especially in England and America, have proved remarkably adroit in discovering pretexts for sidestepping these issues entirely.

TRADITIONAL SOLUTIONS

Traditional solutions fall into three groups, which for lack of more appropriate labels I shall call Christian, Platonic, and intuitionist. The Christian and Platonic solutions are alike in that both involve a denial of the existence of genuine conflicts between the interests of the individual, when these are properly understood, and the interests of the community. This is not to say that Christians and Platonists overlook the obvious fact that individuals do *often* stand to profit *in some ways* from behavior that is detrimental to the well-being of the community.

Their point is rather that although socially undesirable behavior often leads to the achievement of some of the interests of the individual, it *always* blocks the achievement of the individual's *total* interests. So-called conflicts between the individual and society are genuine in the sense that social well-being frequently requires the individual to sacrifice some immediate or partial interest; but in the larger and more accurate sense of the term they are never genuine, since ultimately, all things considered, the interests of the individual coincide with the interests of the community. The appearance of ultimate conflict arises either from our tendency to focus undue attention upon the individual's short-term interests as opposed to his long-term interests or else from our tendency to overestimate certain values, usually "grosser" values such as wealth, pleasure, or prestige, and to underestimate or to ignore other, usually more refined and "higher," values. Of course, just as Platonists and Christians admit that socially unacceptable behavior does often lead to the satisfaction of some partial goals of the individual, so their opponents concede that behavior leading to the satisfaction of an individual's partial or immediate interests often fails to promote his over-all or long-term interests. A commonplace but classic example is that of the dishonest merchant who succeeds in cheating his clients but who is penalized by a ruinous drop in the volume of his business or a powerful crisis of conscience. The question accordingly is the extent to which socially undesirable behavior might promote the over-all, long-term interests of the individual.

The typical Christian philosopher has argued that the individual who engages in antisocial behavior in the belief that it will promote his best interests has simply failed to take into account the penalties for this behavior, if not in this life, then in the next. This solution is admirably simple, and for those who believe firmly in the existence of a divinely appointed system of rewards and punishments after death, it is not without other merits. Since, however, the belief in rewards and punishments after death is avowedly a simple article of faith and since most of us today are reluctant to base our moral convictions upon a totally unprovable assumption, this position will not detain us here. For the sake of accuracy, however, let me point out that this solution, which I have named "Christian," is not supported by all persons who accept this title. Many Christians regard eternal bliss as an arbitrary gift of God or as a privilege due to baptism and repentance for sin rather than as a reward for virtue.

The classic formulation of the Platonic position is found in *The Republic,* the most widely read of Plato's dialogues. Through Socrates, Plato says that the virtuous life is a life devoted to the service of the community; just as health is the good par excellence of the body, so virtue is the good par excellence of the soul. Though the practice of virtue may sometimes cause us to lose other goods, especially wealth, pleasures, or honor, these other values, even taken collectively, cannot outweigh the intrinsic worth of virtue itself. Plato's expression "health of the soul" is, however, intolerably vague, and no one could say with confidence precisely what incomparable and superlative value Plato wished to designate by it. Presumably Plato had in mind a sense of well-being or satisfaction derived from a life of service to one's community or from doing what one believes is right. So stated, however, his position loses whatever plausibility it may initially have had. There can be hardly any doubt that most persons do experience satisfactions of the kind in question and that these satisfactions will often, if taken into account, tip the scales in favor of socially desirable behavior. But most of us would seriously question whether these satisfactions are usually very intense and whether in the experience of some persons they exist at all. It would seem that nothing but the incomparable literary skill of Plato and the desperation with which philosophers have sought a favorable solution to the thorny problem of conflict between private and public interest can account for this argument's ever having appeared to be a solution to large numbers of intelligent persons.

In order to understand the intuitionist position, it will be necessary to make clear two assumptions that underlie both the Platonic and Christian views. One of these assumptions is that the individual has a moral obligation to promote, or at least not to impede, the general welfare. The other is that in order to justify a claim of moral obligation it is necessary to show that its observance will advance the interests of the individual. Now, it will readily be seen why the moral philosopher who makes these two assumptions will want to demonstrate an ultimate coincidence between private and social interest. It will also be seen without difficulty that if one insists upon the individual's moral obligation to society while at the same time denying the ultimate coincidence of private and social interest, consistency requires that one also deny the necessity of supporting claims of moral obligation by showing that it is advantageous for the individual to observe them. And it is precisely this latter denial that most clearly marks those who advance the third, or intuitionist,[1] solution to our problem. According to intuitionists, moral rules are to be observed not because they have desirable consequences for the individual or because the individual experiences a sense of well-being in observing them, but for the simple and sufficient reason that we know them to be valid. If there is a conflict between a moral duty that has the effect of promoting the interests of society and the ultimate best interests of the individual, the individual ought to sacrifice his personal well-being or happiness solely because it is his duty to do so. The Christians tell us to do our duty because by so doing we will go to heaven. Plato told us to do our duty because virtue is its own reward. The intuitionists tell us to do our duty because it is our duty.

The differences between Christians and Platonists, on the one hand, and intuitionists, on the other, are actually more far-reaching than would be supposed from what has just been said. The intuitionists, who appeared relatively late in the history of moral philosophy, not only introduced a new "solution" to this central problem of conflict of interests in moral philosophy but also

[1] The term "intuitionist" is being used here in a narrower sense than is customary. In technical philosophical parlance the position we are describing would be called "deontological intuitionism" to distinguish it from "teleological intuitionism." The deontological intuitionist says that we intuit the validity of statements expressing what constitutes our duty; whereas the teleological intuitionist says we intuit the nature of the good or that which it is our duty to promote. Teleological intuitionism is discussed in Chapter III.

gave to moral philosophy a radically new orientation. For Christians and Platonists, moral philosophy posed three basic problems. The first was to define, or to sharpen, the concept of the good, or the good life; that is to say, to explain as concretely as possible what constitutes individual happiness and social welfare. The second was to sharpen and elaborate the concept of duty, or right conduct; more specifically, to show what kinds of behavior lead to personal happiness and to social well-being, right conduct having been defined, at least implicitly, as conduct with the effect of producing the good. Third, the moral philosopher had either to show that conduct that promotes the social welfare also promotes the happiness of the individual or else to explain how an individual ought to behave when this is not so. We have already seen how Christians and Platonists "solved" this last problem, but what is important to note here is that as long as the problem of determining our duty is identical with the problem of determining what behavior promotes the good, knowledge of our duty need not be considered radically different from any other form of causal knowledge. One could, in principle at least, discover what constitutes duty, or right conduct, by essentially the same kind of empirical or factual inquiry as one would institute to discover what kind of knives cut best or what kind of economic organization leads to the highest level of productivity.

When, however, duty, or right conduct, is no longer defined as that which promotes the good, the methods of ordinary empirical inquiry are no longer relevant. Observation through the physical senses and inductive generalization are no longer helpful. One must discover one's duty by the use of a special intuitive faculty. Moral knowledge will have to be regarded as totally different in kind from knowledge of empirical fact. And instead of the three basic problems stated above, the moral philosopher is faced with two wholly different ones. The first is to clarify the notion of intuitive moral knowledge and to prove that such knowledge exists. The second is to show the extent to which this knowledge can or should influence conduct. The first of these problems is extremely acute in an age that has become increasingly positivistic. And the second is hardly less difficult, as is evidenced by the fact that most intuitionists do not get beyond the bare statement that one ought to do one's duty because it is one's duty—a statement that seems to most of us completely unenlightening. It is, therefore, not altogether surprising that contemporary philosophers have increasingly rejected the notion of moral knowledge altogether, classifying statements about right and wrong as primarily expressions of approval or disapproval.

To avoid possible misunderstanding, let me emphasize that the purpose of the preceding remarks has not been to prove, even in any loose sense of the term, that the positions discussed are false. That a theory does not appeal to large numbers of contemporary thinkers is entirely compatible with its being true, as far as logic is concerned. The intent has been simply to give the reader some notion of the historical background of the problem to which this chapter is dedicated and to explain the pragmatic need for a fresh solution. A more detailed treatment of the traditional positions will be found in subsequent chapters.

AN ALTERNATIVE SOLUTION

As we have seen, Platonists and Christians defined right conduct as conduct that promotes the good, and they distinguished two species of the good—individual well-being and social well-being. From this definition and distinction, the following questions arose: Can an act be right if it does not simultaneously promote both species of good? Conversely, can an act be wrong if it promotes either species of good? To both of these questions the answers were "no." Philosophers in the Platonic-Christian tradition were not, however, altogether comfortable about their answers; for if private and public good do not ultimately coincide, then some acts that are ordinarily regarded as wrong might not properly be so regarded. If, for instance, it were in a man's ultimate best interests to steal, then stealing under these circumstances would not be wrong, and the man could not legitimately be censured for stealing. To avoid this awkward consequence, these philosophers declared that there is no ultimate conflict between private and public interest, because it is always in the ultimate best interests of the individual to observe society's moral rules.

Now, my own position is in many respects similar to that of the Platonists and Christians. Like them, I regard right conduct as conduct that simultaneously promotes public and private good. Like them, I refuse to regard conduct that promotes only private or only public good as wrong. And although I do not share their confident conviction that there never is or can be an ultimate conflict between private and social good, I am *not* convinced that conflicts of this kind ever do occur, and I *am* convinced that if they do they occur much more rarely than is generally supposed.

The chief, and by no means negligible, difference between their position and mine is as follows. Platonists and Christians explained the widespread belief in the noncoincidence of public and private interests as the result of a failure properly to understand personal well-being. They argued that the individual promotes social welfare by a rigid adherence to the conventional moral code and that the individual will be rewarded for this conduct either immediately, in this life, or in an afterlife. When, therefore, an apparent conflict between the individual and society arose, the individual was requested to acquiesce for his own good. According to my position, the general disbelief in substantial coincidence of private and public good usually arises, on the contrary, from an improper understanding of what promotes the general welfare, which may sometimes be advanced by an individual's deliberate disregard of conventional moral rules. When, therefore, an apparent conflict between the individual and society arises, society ought often to bend for society's sake. To put this difference in other terms, whereas Platonic-Christian thinkers were essentially conservative and tended to construe social welfare almost exclusively in terms of order, or stability, my position allows a greater place for social progress.

Formally, the position I wish to argue for in this chapter may be stated in the following terms: A man is legitimately subject to moral censure for performing an act only if he has good reason to regard that act as detrimental to his own best long-range interests, whereas a man is entitled to moral commendation for performing an act only if he has good reason to regard that act as conducive to his own best long-range interests. The defense of this position, very briefly stated, is that the general adoption of this policy for the distribution of praise and blame serves not only the interests of the individual but also the interests of the community. Three arguments will be presented in defense of this view. In order to follow these arguments more easily, it will be helpful to keep the two following hypothetical cases in mind.

A person of low intelligence and repulsive physical features from a slum district in one of our larger cities grows up in a poverty-stricken, broken home, neglected by his parents and despised by those around him. He resorts to theft, believing for good reasons that he will probably not be caught or that even life in jail is preferable to the life to which he has otherwise been condemned. Now, according to the traditional view, the interests of society would best be served in this case by a generous use of moral censure. According to my view, the interests of society can not be served in this way. It is even likely that society would benefit by praising the man.

Again, we have a man of low intelligence and repulsive physical features from a slum district. Again, he grows up in a poverty-stricken, broken home, neglected by his parents and despised by those around him. This time, however, we shall endow him with an intuition that one ought to sacrifice one's own welfare to that of others, with a hope that he will be rewarded in an afterlife for so doing, or, finally, with a belief that "virtue is its own reward." He thus drudges away a weary existence, eking out an "honest living" for himself and three abandoned nephews whom he loathes, refusing to indulge his appetites for women, drink, and decent food—almost the only pleasures that, given his background, he is capable of enjoying. According to the traditional view, this man ought to be praised. In my view, society cannot expect to benefit by praising this man. In all likelihood social interests require that he be censured.

The first argument in support of the position adopted here turns on the belief that most socially dangerous acts have their source in impulsive and ill-considered action, for which the corrective is deliberate and rational pursuit of true self-interest. As many traditional philosophers have pointed out, morality requires more, not less, regard for our own all-round personal well-being. Since, however, the only grounds they have ever given for putting social welfare above one's own long-range interests are the beliefs that there are rewards and punishments after death, that no reasons are required beyond intuition of some allegedly impersonal moral law, and that virtue is its own reward, they have tacitly sanctioned faith, intuition, and confidence in a thoroughly implausible psychological generalization as legitimate motives for behavior. The result has been that those who pride themselves on their rationality often tend to develop contempt for conventional moral rules, while those who pride themselves on their moral earnestness often tend to develop contempt for reason. The danger to social well-being in the first case is obvious; and although the danger in the second case is less obvious, it is no less serious. One cannot lose respect for reason without weakening one's precious but usually feeble habits of rational self-control. A man who is taught to accept faith or intuition as legitimate bases of belief cannot be expected to develop a healthy respect for rationality, and neither can a man who is taught not to question psychological generalizations simply because they appear initially to favor "virtue." Our cognitive life is not easily compartmentalized, and who or what will adjudicate the disputes that arise when faith or intuition inclines us to one belief and reason to a different belief? On the other hand, by praising a man for acting consistently in his own best interests one encourages him to cultivate habits of rationality and rational self-control with all of the social advantages which this entails.

Second, it frequently happens that in the long and complex chain of causes culminating in antisocial behavior the most significant are individual attitudes or dispositions which society can effectively control by the use of moral sanctions. This is especially the case when the behavior is inspired by disregard of individual self-interest. It also and by no means infrequently happens that the significant causal factors are not personal attitudes or dispositions but rather social institutions or circumstances which can be effectively counteracted only by concerted social action. This, I maintain, is almost invariably the case when an individual has been led to perform a socially undesirable act because the prevailing system of rewards and penalties renders that act in his own best all-round interests. Since, however, by blaming a man for his behavior we usually imply that the principal source of the difficulty lies within him and can best be corrected by him, we cannot urge the individual to put the social welfare above his own best long-range interests without tending to divert attention from the social causes of his embarrassment and fixing upon him individually a responsibility that belongs to all of us collectively as members of society.

A related distinction is between blaming an individual for performing an act with socially undesirable effects and blaming society for a complacent tolerance of the conditions that led him to perform the act. Although in some cases this is wholly or very nearly an either-or proposition, it would be a mistake to suppose that the occurrence of a socially injurious act ought never to serve as an occasion for blaming both the individual who performed it *and* society. In many cases both reproaches would be justified. To the extent that the socially undesirable act is not in the best interests of the agent, the agent ought to be blamed for performing it. To the extent that the act is produced by conditions that others would find it in their own best interests to eliminate, they ought to be blamed. The point is simply that the criterion by which we decide which reproach is legitimate or how much weight should be accorded to each ought to be the best long-range interests of the individuals concerned. The disinterested altruist who preaches the sacrifice of the individual in the name of society allows little, if any, place for efforts at social reform and undermines the individual's sense of his own dignity and personal worth. At the opposite extreme old-style social reformers and humanitarians have all too readily adopted some scheme of social or economic determinism that gives us little, if any, hold upon the individual and jeopardizes the concept of individual moral responsibility altogether.[2]

Despite the influence of this latter group, however, we still tend overmuch to focus blame upon the individual agent rather than society whenever the agent performs an act with socially undesirable consequences. There are three principal reasons for this. First, the agent has in almost all cases of the kind under consideration here performed an act that most persons would not have found it in their own best interests to perform, and we do not always appreciate the unusual circumstances that obtain in a particular case. Second, although social institutions or circumstances are as important to a causal understanding of socially undesirable behavior as individual attitudes or personality traits, the latter, being more immediate and often more dramatically interesting causes, tend to crowd the former out of mind. This is especially true in a highly moralistic, apolitical, and psychologically oriented society such as our own. Third, moral indignation is usually accompanied by a pleasing sentiment of superiority and can often serve as a mask for our own shortsightedness and complacency with respect to social injustice. But this tendency to blame the agent rather than society is often in conflict with our desire for a more equitable and harmonious social order and must be controlled in our own best long-range interests.

The simple fact is that moral censure is not often an effective means of promoting the general welfare when an individual performs an act dictated by rational consideration of his own best long-range interests. If we succeed in persuading the individual that he is at fault in so acting, it will probably be at the cost of jeopardizing his and our own rational habits. If we do not succeed, we will probably embitter the offender of the conventional code and reinforce his antisocial attitudes. The best thing to do at

[2] I do not mean to suggest by this remark that moral responsibility implies indeterminism. My own position is antagonistic to libertarianism, as will be made clear in Chapter VII. At this point I am merely registering a protest against certain crude forms of determinism according to which moral sanctions are causally inefficacious in producing desirable human behavior.

this point if we wish to promote the general welfare is to remind ourselves of the social imperfections that have given rise to the conflict and to censure ourselves and others for having tolerated the conditions producing these tragic cases.

When, on the other hand, we praise an individual for acting consistently in his own best long-range interests even though this sometimes involves the performance of socially disapproved behavior, we not only encourage the individual violently to protest against the injustices of which he is a victim, but we also protest against these injustices ourselves in a highly dramatic way. Some persons will, no doubt, regard this remedy as unduly drastic. In the example above, it would involve condoning the agent if he abandoned his nephews and took to theft, since by hypothesis theft is in his own best long-range interests. If we remember, however, (a) that the alternative to deliberate pursuit of long-range self-interest is abject acquiescence to social injustice and impoverishment of the human personality and (b) that we ordinarily postulate as the goal of the moral life the greatest possible coincidence of private and social welfare not merely in the present but in the future as well, then my position is very difficult to refute.

Third, and finally, there is the following argument. In distributing praise and blame according to how a man acts or fails to act in his own best long-range interests, we oblige ourselves to take the interests of other individuals into fuller consideration than we would if we distributed praise and blame in some other fashion, thereby eliminating a very considerable source of friction and bitterness in human relationships. As we saw earlier, the probable effect of urging a man to act contrary to what he rationally regards as his own best interests is either to embitter him or to inspire contempt for reason. The probable effect of urging a man consistently to act in his own best rational interests, however, is to establish a relationship of mutual respect with him, thus creating conditions that favor a reasonable and co-operative endeavor to reconcile differing interests and disposing the agent to regard with greater sympathy moral rules designed to promote the general welfare. A man whom fortune has not favored is far more likely to co-operate with others and far less likely to adopt a solution to his problems that runs counter to their interests if he knows that they are acutely aware of his misfortune and are acting to ameliorate his lot.

ANSWERS TO OBJECTIONS

Both the statement of the position and the arguments presented on its behalf in the preceding section are open to a number of misinterpretations and objections, which, because of their complexity or for the sake of expository convenience, will be dealt with in chapters that follow. A few misunderstandings and difficulties, however, can be profitably discussed now.

1. Many persons will object to the moral program recommended on the grounds that it is excessively indulgent. Whatever else the moral life involves, it involves sacrifice and discipline. Making the individual's own self-interest a criterion for deciding moral obligation is, they will say, an instance of weak-kneed sentimentality. It must, however, be noted that the moral demand on the individual is not simply to pursue his self-interest, but *rationally* to pursue his self-interest. Rationality is one of the key concepts in this study, and much more will be said on this subject in later chapters. But let it be said now that rationality is a discipline requiring great effort and many sacrifices.

2. In defending the claim that the individual ought not to be blamed for acting in his own best self-interest even at the expense of others, it was argued that society has an obligation to the individual. Strictly speaking, of course, only individuals have obligations: to say that society has an obligation to the individual is simply to say that individuals have obligations to one another. Moreover, within the framework of the position just outlined, any obligation to others must be such that it can be derived from an obligation to oneself. What, then, is the nature of an individual's obligation to others, how far does that obligation extend, and how can the claim that such an obligation exists be justified? These questions are perfectly legitimate because social

welfare is, for most of us, at least, as important a criterion of right conduct as personal well-being. In answering them, let us make three assumptions. First, practically all individuals desire an environment in which their own goals and those of others may be harmoniously realized, not only because social harmony makes it easier for us to attain individual goals but also because where our private interests are not affected we usually prefer the happiness of others to their misery. Second, the desire for social harmony would be considerably stronger if only we were fully rational and thus more aware than most of us are of the extent to which personal unhappiness derives from social circumstance. Third, it is not only within the power of every individual to do something toward creating a more favorable social environment than presently exists, but also with rare exceptions it would be in the best rational interest of the individual to do so. An individual's obligation to others is thus a function of his desire to eliminate actual or possible sources of conflict together with the necessity he is under to co-operate with others in order to achieve that goal. The extent of his obligation is a function of the number of possible sources of painful conflict, the degree of his dependence upon others, and the extent to which conditions permit him to promote social reforms.

3. It was earlier stated that although my position does imply a greater coincidence between private and public good than is usually supposed to exist, it does not necessarily imply a perfect, or invariable, coincidence between private and public good. But, it might be asked, if the coincidence between private and public good is not perfect, how can you recommend praise for those who follow self-interest at the expense of society or blame for those who follow the opposite course? To this question the answer is that no such policy is recommended. My position is that self-interest is a *necessary* condition of morally correct behavior, not a *sufficient* condition. Moreover, as I said above, social well-being is an equally necessary condition. If a case should arise in which an individual must choose between serving the public interest at the expense of his personal well-being or promoting his private interest at the expense of society, his choice, whatever it might

be, would, on my view, merit neither praise nor blame. The person who faces such a choice and the second parties who would like to advise him are confronted by an insoluble moral dilemma. We cannot praise a man for an act unless it is right, but an act is not right unless it promotes both the interests of the agent and the interests of the community. We cannot blame a man for an act unless it is wrong, but an act is not wrong unless it fails to promote either his own personal interests or the interests of the community. The humanly appropriate reaction when we discover a case of ultimate conflict between private and social interest, if we ever do, is to dedicate ourselves to preventing the recurrence of similar situations rather than to attempt the impossible task of moral appraisal of the individual involved.

Fortunately, as the arguments presented in the last section were designed to make clear, such socially valuable consequences usually follow from a consistently rational pursuit of self-interest that in any reasonably well-ordered society cases of ultimate conflict between the individual and society are either nonexistent or exceedingly rare. It is only in a very imperfectly ordered society where rewards for socially valuable behavior or penalties for its opposite are virtually nonexistent and where the social conscience is so poorly developed that the society's members are unwilling to make any serious effort to correct the situation that ultimate conflicts between the individual and society are likely to occur.

4. Since on my view self-interest is a necessary rather than a sufficient condition of morally correct behavior, I am not formally committed to the thesis that in every instance where self-interest requires the violation of established moral rules the individual who follows self-interest is to be praised. In arguing, however, that behavior in accordance with self-interest does almost invariably promote the social good in any reasonably well-ordered society, I do imply that the individual who violates established moral rules when self-interest requires it ought to be praised in the vast majority of cases. Now, many persons who will readily agree that an individual ought not to be blamed in cases of this kind will balk at the view that he ought to be praised, even though they accept my contention with regard to the ultimate

social benefits following from a consistent pursuit of self-interest. An act, they will say, is not praiseworthy simply because it has desirable consequences; it must also be performed from morally acceptable motives. And although in the past most philosophers regarded prudence or concern for one's own well-being as a perfectly acceptable moral motive, we have come increasingly in the last century to make a sharp distinction between prudential and moral motives.

If, for instance, a civil rights worker violated a law, believing rightly that violation of this law was necessary to eradicate grave social injustice and for that reason alone, most of us would praise him. If, however, he performed the same act for reasons of pure self-interest, many of us would not praise him. We would not do so even though we believed that the social effects of his act were on the whole good.

As I will make clear in later chapters, benevolent, altruistic motives are morally superior to prudential ones. Consequently, I appreciate our relative reluctance to praise a man when his act is performed from the latter rather than the former kind of motives. None the less, I cannot understand why prudence or rational consideration of self-interest should be unacceptable as a moral motive. If the argument up to this point is correct, prudence is definitely a trait from which society profits. To sneer at it or to refuse to acknowledge its moral value would be comparable to sneering at or refusing to admire the work of a minor artist because he is not a major artist.

5. It was earlier maintained that moral blame is never a legitimate form of punishment if the individual has acted rationally in his own best long-range interests. Some might feel that this is to deprive society of one of its best and most effective modes of punishment in cases where punishment is most needed. If an individual finds it in his own best interests to flout the conventional moral code, this may be either because society has not sufficiently rewarded him for observing the code or because society has not imposed sufficient penalties, including moral censure, for violations of the code. When, therefore, as in the illustrative example, an individual finds it in his own best long-range interests to

violate the code, it is partly because these violations are not regarded with sufficient gravity, and this may rightly be taken as a cue for the imposition of stronger sanctions by way of moral censure in the future.

In answer to this objection it must be granted that if crime had been punished by stronger moral censure the hero in our example might not have found it in his own self-interest to resort to theft. It must also be granted that facts of this kind may often be legitimately used to establish the need to impose stronger moral sanctions in the future. But these admissions do not in any way jeopardize my original position. In the first place, we often fail to distinguish between acts subject to moral censure or approval and acts of moral censure or approval themselves. If stronger moral sanctions would prevent individuals from performing antisocial acts, this might well be a reason for adopting stronger sanctions in the future and for blaming those who did not impose sufficiently strong moral sanctions in the past. But reasons for imposing stronger sanctions for a particular type of socially injurious act in the future or for blaming those who did not impose such sanctions in the past are not necessarily reasons for blaming an agent who has just performed that type of act. In the second place, we often tend to forget that moral sanctions are not usually effective unless they can be justified by an appeal to self-interest. It is true that some persons are so anxious for the good will and approbation of others that they will submit to any taboo, however irrational, rather than risk the loss of this good will and approbation. It is also true that almost all men have a moderately strong impulse to avoid the performance of acts that might arouse disapproval simply for the sake of avoiding disapproval and that as long as the cost is slight they ordinarily act upon this impulse. But it is no less true that a moral injunction usually has little or no effect upon an individual who clearly sees great advantages to be gained by circumventing it.

6. It is sometimes said that if one cannot justify the imposition of moral sanctions one cannot justify the imposition of sanctions of other types. If, for instance, one cannot legitimately blame an individual for performing a theft, one cannot legitimately im-

prison him. The difficulty here is due to a simple confusion between a moral right to impose any sanction and a moral right to impose a moral sanction; for although one is expected morally to justify the imposition of any sanction by showing that it is in the interests of society to do so, it does not follow that it will always be in the interests of society to impose a moral sanction whenever it is in the interests of society to impose a penal or an economic sanction. If the Americans and the Russians could intelligibly debate the relative merits of penal and economic sanctions for war criminals, there is no reason why moral philosophers cannot discuss the relative merits of moral sanctions as opposed to other types of sanctions.

To be sure, it has been argued that one reason for praising a man who violates the established legal code when this is in his own best long-term interests is that by so doing we dispose others to alter the social conditions that made it in his interests to perform the act. And it might be countered that an even more effective way of doing this is to refuse to imprison men in such cases. However, the balance between the socially valuable and the socially injurious aspects of this latter course is so wholly different from that of the former that nobody would want seriously to consider it. Furthermore, the law-breaker who is imprisoned for the protection of others can more easily appreciate the motives that led to his incarceration than he can the automatic contempt or moral disapproval of those who make no effort to understand the circumstances that led him to act as he did. It is certainly not unreasonable to suppose, as many social workers have claimed, that a fairly large number of criminals who might otherwise have returned from prison better men than when they entered became instead so embittered by the unreasoning and blind contempt to which they are often subject that reform was no longer possible.

7. Many persons find a certain splendor in acts of self-sacrifice that are not in the agent's best long-range interests, especially when these acts are dictated by a sense of duty or an attitude of benevolence.[3] These persons will object violently to withholding

[3] For a concrete analysis of the sense of duty and the spirit of benevolence and of the role they play in the moral life, see Chapters II and VII.

moral commendation for such acts. Now, this objection raises issues that cannot be adequately dealt with at this point. It will, however, be helpful to observe that many of these acts retain their splendor even for someone who accepts my point of view. This would be the case, for instance, when the act follows from a sense of duty or an attitude of benevolence that was itself rationally cultivated in the belief it was in the agent's best over-all interests and that has become a permanent personality trait over which the agent has little conscious control. In a case of this kind, the person has simply acted on the basis of probable knowledge that turned out to be false in much the same way that one makes a reasonable bet and loses. Consider, for example, someone who has developed a habit of civic responsibility which, because of a war that could not reasonably have been anticipated, turns out to be contrary to his best interests. If the sense of civic responsibility was so deeply rooted that the man could not adjust to the new conditions, we would tend to regard him as a magnificent witness to the grandeur of a more decent age. But since a rationally cultivated sense of duty or habit of benevolence is almost always subject to some measure of conscious control, our attitude here is usually ambivalent—which adds weight to the position taken in this book. Think here of one's reaction to the German or Frenchman who out of a sense of duty refused to participate in the black market during the lean years after World War II and who as a consequence starved to death. Our admiration is not usually unalloyed. To the extent that we suspect this behavior to reflect a willful disregard of self-interest, our admiration is more often than not tempered by pity or contempt.

8. It might be said that but for the heroic, unrewarded sacrifices of martyrs and the benefits conferred upon society by the fanatical zeal of social reformers who have been too rash to consult their own interests civilization would never have emerged and would soon disappear. There seems, however, to be no historical warrant for such a claim. Regardless of what one's criteria of historical progress may be, one is almost forced to the conclusion that the martyr and the fanatic have done at least as much harm as good and that their influence has rarely if ever been historically

decisive, since every cause has produced its own martyrs and fanatics. It was not, for instance, because there were so few martyrs and heroes that Nazism developed in Germany. The Nazis demonstrated a capacity for martyrdom and heroism which was probably not surpassed by that of the non-Nazis. It would seem rather that Nazism developed largely because the English and the French in 1917 and the Germans again in 1933 preferred the immediate pleasures of self-righteous indignation and revenge to the rational pursuit of long-range self-interest. Similarly, it is not because there are so few martyrs and heroes that academic freedom is jeopardized in the United States today. It is rather because so many professors prefer an immediate advantage in the form of rapid promotion or harmonious relations with administrative authorities to the long-range advantages of an easy conscience and genuine freedom.

Granting that our argument up to this point is correct, it follows that if each of us were prepared to make reasonable sacrifices for the sake of more or less distant personal goods, the result would be a state of society in which private and social interests tend to coincide, thus eliminating the "need" for anyone to make unreasonable sacrifices for the good of others. But, as long as morality remains chained to Christian ideals, it will, like the Christian God, be forever divided between the claims of justice and the claims of charity unless in an effort to satisfy each it is forced to sacrifice both.

9. Although we all find situations in which private and social interests conflict more or less painful and although it is clear upon reflection that the only genuinely satisfactory method for eliminating such situations is social improvement, the burden of improving society is often a heavy one, requiring the sacrifice of immediate to future satisfactions. Many of us would like to believe that there are other and easier methods, either through religious faith or through some form of personal hygiene or moral asceticism. That such methods are effective ways of handling these conflicts is an almost patently false proposition, though many powerful idols of the theater are invoked to give it credence. In particular, there are the philosophical doctrine of disinterested

altruism and the religious doctrine that this is the best of all possible worlds, together with its secular version, the philosophy of "adjustment," which often accompanies it.

Moreover, many men have a vested interest in the *status quo* and would rather suffer the pangs of a guilty conscience and circumscribe the range of their human sympathies than risk endangering certain sources of satisfaction that depend upon the preservation of the *status quo*. These men, whose power over public opinion through the churches, the schools, the newspapers and other mass media of communication is out of all proportion to their numbers, lend their support to the idols of the theater mentioned above either for the purpose of silencing those who threaten their position or in order to assuage their own consciences. Now, as long as the nature of these powerful psychological and sociological props of traditional morality go unrecognized, no rational arguments in support of my position, however sound, will be able to blot out the psychological disturbance that most of us feel when we first entertain it.

chapter two

CONSCIENCE

According to the arguments presented in Chapter I cases of ultimate conflict between the individual and society are rare or nonexistent, and even if a case of ultimate conflict occurs, an individual cannot be said to be acting wrongly if he pursues his own welfare. Self-interest thus becomes a serviceable criterion for identifying morally objectionable behavior. Even an individual's obligations to society are deducible from this criterion, it being the duty of the individual to promote the well-being of others if and only if it is in his interest to do so. If follows that the practical problem for the individual moral agent who wishes to avoid wrong-doing in any concrete situation of moral perplexity is to determine what course of action promotes his own best interests. In other words, to avoid wrong-doing it suffices that the individual acquire as full and accurate knowledge as possible of his own basic desires as well as the means of fulfilling them and that he allow this knowledge to guide his conduct. The recommended method for the acquisition of relevant moral knowledge is intelligent common sense or scientific inquiry.

This position clashes violently with that of the intuitionists. These philosophers say that an act is right or wrong, not because of its tendency to promote or impede human well-being, but rather because it is known to be right or wrong by a special faculty of the mind or soul. Although some intuitionists, especially contemporary ones, do not often use the term, this faculty is most often called "conscience," and it is by this name that I shall designate it in this study. These intuitionists would most especially challenge the role attributed to desire in my theory.

For them conscience is a distinct human faculty endowed with a knowledge of right and wrong and capable of competing with desire for the privilege of influencing conduct. Conscience, they say, stands in opposition to desire. Desire has its source within ourselves; conscience speaks with another voice. Desire has to do with satisfactions and dissatisfactions; conscience, with right and wrong. Desire is personal; conscience, impersonal. Desire calls only for gratification, conscience often demands self-sacrifice.

Apart from the impossibility of squaring the intuitionist interpretation of moral experience with the persistent demand that adherence to moral rules be justified by showing that the individual will ultimately profit from them, intuitionism poses two other difficulties. The first is to give a satisfactory account of the nature of the knowledge conscience allegedly delivers. The knowledge of right and wrong as perceived by conscience is a mysterious type of knowledge and extremely difficult to characterize concretely. Christians often call conscience the voice of God in man. For others, especially Kant, conscience is the voice of the "noumenal self," *i.e.*, a nonempirical self that can be neither perceived nor introspected and whose existence is merely postulated. For still others, notably Plato, conscience appears to be a vision of eternal, transcendent ideas of right and wrong. Moreover, no intuitionist has ever given a clear criterion for distinguishing between true and false conscience, between genuinely authoritative pronouncements and socially indoctrinated prejudice.

The second difficulty concerns the manner in which conscience supposedly influences behavior. Ordinarily its influence upon conduct is said to be mediated through an act of free will. But the concept of free will is no less opaque than that of the knowledge that conscience supposedly delivers and in any case suggests more problems than it solves, as I shall try to show in Chapter VII.

That my own views escape these difficulties is perfectly clear. The knowledge relevant to the moral life on my account is ordinary empirical knowledge. And since this knowledge is knowledge of what constitutes the well-being of society and of the individual agent—forms of well-being that are actually desired—there is no puzzle involved in the assertion that such knowledge can move us to act. There are, however, two objections to my position that stem very naturally from the intuitionist interpretation of the moral life. One is that I cannot give an adequate explanation of the states of mind familiarly described as conflicts between conscience and desire (or duty and desire) and that an attempt to do so would inevitably lead either to a confusion between simple frustration and genuine moral conflict or else to a reduction of the moral life to a crude mechanical hedonistic calculus. The second objection is either that I cannot explain the motivation of heroic acts of self-sacrifice or that if I did it would only be possible by depriving these acts of their moral worth.

TERMINOLOGICAL CLARIFICATIONS

To deal adequately with these two objections, a few of the crucial terms used in answering them must be explained. One is "desire," which I shall be using exclusively to refer to an actually introspectable state of consciousness. In a typical, or paradigm, case of desire the following elements exist: (a) representation of a goal, (b) belief that the envisaged goal is attainable without undue strain, (c) belief that the envisaged goal, if brought into being, will provide the agent a felt satisfaction, (d) an affective state or feeling, usually a feeling of pleasure by way of anticipation, which disposes us to seek out the envisaged goal, and (e) belief that the dissatisfactions, if any, consequent upon the performance of actions leading to the attainment of the envisaged goal are not such as to offset the satisfactions involved in its attainment.

Of these five factors, the first four are clearly essential to any case of desire. If there were no conscious representation of a possible future state, one would hardly be tempted to speak of a desire since this would involve the almost self-contradictory notion of a desire without an object, a desire that is not the desire of something. If the conscious representation of a goal were not accompanied by a belief in its attainability, the agent would wish rather than desire. One does not, for instance, desire to jump over the moon, but the child in his fancy might wish to do so. If there were no belief that the envisaged situation would be a source of satisfaction, the conscious state of the agent would have to be described by some such term as "indifference," "aversion," or "curiosity" rather than by "desire." Finally, if there were no affective element, or positive feeling tone, the state of mind would lack that very element which is most distinctive of desire.

The fifth factor, however, is not a necessary ingredient of desire. It frequently happens that conditions (a), (b), (c), and (d) are satisfied and that the agent acts on the desire so constituted while being firmly convinced that the satisfactions involved in the attainment of the end-in-view *are* offset by attendant dissatisfactions. Let us use the term "compulsion" to describe these cases. Although desire is often confused with compulsion (and, as will be seen later, not without good reason), they are distinguishable. The alcoholic, the dope addict, and the sex fiend almost always insist that they do not desire the drink, the dope, or the sexual experience toward which their actions are oriented but rather are compelled, or forced, to orient their actions toward these goals. Typically they claim to know, and in fact do know, that their actions impede the attainment of their best over-all interests.

It has frequently been asked how compulsion is possible.[1] How can a person do what he knows is not in his best long-range interests? The problem is as old as Socrates. He held that if a man *really* knew that the more remote consequences of his act would be injurious to him and render the satisfaction involved in the attainment of the more immediate end-in-view not worthwhile, then he could not perform the act. In other words he said that compulsion is impossible. This problem is partially solved once we recognize that the motive of conscious and deliberate behavior usually includes not only abstract beliefs as to what is in one's

[1] In the discussion that follows I have made no attempt to give a fully adequate explanation of compulsive behavior but only to indicate some of its more prominent features in typical cases. In particular, I do not profess to understand or to explain those forms of behavior such as kleptomania or compulsive handwashing that psychiatrists attribute to obsessional neurosis.

best interests but also some felt quality of experience at the moment action is initiated. Alcoholism, for instance, often becomes possible because a man anticipates and feels the satisfactions of drinking more vividly and more concretely than the more remote consequences of his act. This explains why a trip through an alcoholic ward or some other means of rendering the more remote consequences of drinking concrete and readily imaginable has a deterrent effect upon the formation of such a compulsive habit, although, of course, it has little or no effect once the habit has been formed. What Socrates did not seem adequately to recognize in most of his work is that "really know" in such contexts means "know concretely." For Socrates the proper objects of real knowledge were eternal ideas; in fact, the proper object of real knowledge is the full, concrete situation. To say that a man knows or believes that the remote, future consequences of his acts entail dissatisfactions such as to offset the satisfaction attending the immediate end-in-view and yet chooses the immediate end-in-view is often to say simply that he has a more concrete and personal knowledge of the immediate satisfaction than he has of the remoter consequences of his acts. We know now that *delirium tremens* is an excruciating experience. We should know this more concretely if we visited an alcoholic ward, and still more concretely if we were to become alcoholics.

This analysis helps us to understand why desire and compulsion are so frequently confused. Since the distinction between abstract and concrete knowledge is largely, if not entirely, a relative one marking off graduations within knowledge in a wider sense, so compulsion and desire may be conceived as gradations within desire in a wider sense of the latter term. To mark the similarities without losing sight of the differences, I shall refer in what follows to more and less concrete or abstract cognitions and to more and less compulsive or noncompulsive desires, thus reinstating the term "desire" in its more traditional and broader meaning. We thus understand how it is possible for a person to do what he does not want or desire to do and yet to be always acting from desire.

The phenomena of fear may be analyzed in a comparable manner. A fear is like a desire except that the envisaged situation is believed to be dissatisfying rather than satisfying, and the felt quality of experience at the moment of initiating action is negative rather than positive. Fears, like desires, may be classified as compulsive or noncompulsive. If, for instance, a man knows that he must undergo an operation to ensure his total well-being but cannot bring himself to go into the hospital, it is usually because he has concrete knowledge of the painfulness of the operation but only abstract knowledge of the future well-being it may promote. His fear is, therefore, compulsive; and the most generally satisfactory technique for overcoming this compulsive fear is for the person to dwell upon the pleasures and satisfactions that are in store once the painful experience has been undergone, thus rendering his knowledge of the long-range consequences of his acts more concrete. It is not surprising that fear and desire permit of similar analyses, since there is no fear without desire. If one fears social disapproval, for instance, one also desires social esteem.

Another key term in the analyses that follow is "habit," by which I understand any reasonably specific response to any reasonably specific stimulus that (a) is recurrent, (b) was initially performed as a result of conscious deliberation or a conscious learning process, and (c) was subsequently performed without conscious deliberation or learning effort. It should be immediately noted that originally conscious behavior regularly tends to become habitual upon repetition and that the more habitual a mode of conduct becomes the more difficult it is, as a rule, for the agent to recall the original conscious process that led to its formation and the less amenable it is to conscious control. These points, innocent and unenlightening though they are in themselves, are important for an understanding of conscience. They also explain why even highly concrete knowledge is often without influence upon conduct, as when the alcoholic with his greater concrete knowledge of the consequences of his acts is none the less unable to stop drinking. The formation of compulsive habits usually depends upon ignorance or failure of concreteness in the apprehension of the consequences of one's acts, but a full and concrete apprehension of the consequences of one's acts is rarely a sufficient condition for breaking compulsive habits already formed.

Finally, it will be necessary to say a word about my use of the expressions "fundamental desire" or "basic desire," terms which will be used synonymously throughout this book. Basic, or fundamental, desires are exceptionally high-order desires that would, if consistently acted upon, exert a pervasive influence over a very wide range of conduct, either aiding us in the achievement of many subsidiary desires or minimizing competition between lower-order desires that cannot be simultaneously realized. Examples of basic desires are the desire for a large stock of funded knowledge, which would obviously be helpful in realizing our more particular goals, and the desire for a state of society in which private and social interests more nearly coincide, since there is no greater obstacle to the achievement of our desires and no greater source of intrapersonal conflict than interpersonal hostilities. Special care must be taken to avoid the confusion between *basic* and *strong* desires. If the strength of a desire is measured either by the amount of affective charge that accompanies it or by the number of times it is actually acted upon, it is evident that many basic desires are relatively weak, almost all human beings having a tendency to pursue concretely envisaged specific goals with greater energy than more generalized but less concretely envisaged goals.

THE CONFLICT BETWEEN DUTY AND DESIRE

The familiar phenomena most frequently described as cases of conflict between conscience and desire do not require for their understanding either a belief in cognitive factors beyond those involved in ordinary empirical knowledge or belief in motivational factors other than those of desire, compulsion, and habit.

The conflict between desire and conscience may take two forms.

The first exhibits a conflict between desire and the "authoritarian" conscience, the second, a conflict between desire and the "humanitarian" conscience.[2] The authoritarian conscience expresses itself in the feeling of indecision and mental distress that frequently overtakes us when we violate a general principle of conduct to which we feel somehow committed and in the regret we experience when we recall the violation. (I mean to include under "violation" the temptation to act out of harmony with the principle as well as the actual performance of the act.) The humanitarian conscience manifests itself in a comparable feeling of indecision, distress, and regret with respect to the performance of acts that we believe to promote our own personal interests at the expense of others.

The authoritarian conscience may be crudely illustrated as follows: A boy desires a favor of his parents and sees a way to obtain the favor through lying. He knows that if he is discovered in the lie, he will incur the disapproval of external authorities—parents, teachers, minister, or playmates—and will be punished by the paddle, by deprivation of privileges, or simply by silent scorn. He is uncomfortable about the situation and indecisive. After a short deliberation, however, he performs the act; and later, even before discovery, he regrets it. As an illustration of the humanitarian conscience, we may take the case of the hero in Arthur Miller's *All My Sons*. The hero is a small wartime industrialist under contract to the government to supply equipment for use in combat airplanes. He supplies defective equipment despite his knowledge that this might well lead to unnecessary casualties. His son, upon return from combat service, gradually discovers his father's crime and turns upon him with mingled hate and contempt. A shot offstage signals the tragic end—suicide.

In examining these cases, I shall attempt to show that their description as conflicts in which desire is set against conscience, as conscience is traditionally understood, is misleading and that they can be fully and far more accurately described as conflicts

[2] These terms have been borrowed from Erich Fromm, *Man for Himself* (New York: Rinehart & Co., Inc., 1948), pp. 143–72. They are not, however, being used in the same sense given them by Fromm.

between specific types of desires, no reference being made to "conscience" either as a motivational or as a cognitive factor in the situation. It is sufficient for this purpose to recognize levels of desire distinguished first by their strength or weakness, second by the range and generality of their goals, and third by the concreteness or abstractness of the knowledge that informs them. The conflict between desire and conscience may thus be interpreted as a conflict between a strong, lower-order, or compulsive, desire, on the one hand, and a more basic, noncompulsive, but weaker desire, on the other. In the examples cited, desire for self-respect or social esteem and familial love or sympathy is pitted against the desire for the favor in the case of the boy and the desire for "success" in the case of the industrialist. It is obvious that for either the boy or the industrialist to have performed the acts that they later regretted, at the moment these acts were performed the end-in-view of the more concrete desire had to hold for them a greater appeal than the end-in-view of the more general desire. In other words, the desire upon which they acted must have been somewhat compulsive in character. Both the boy and the industrialist knew, in the same sense that the alcoholic or the dope addict knows, both the incompatibility of the desires involved and the greater long-range satisfactions afforded by behavior modeled on the generalized abstract desire over behavior modeled on the particular concrete desire. This is especially apparent in the case of the boy—if anyone doubts this analysis, let him discover a typical boy in a typical lie or theft and ask him why he did it. More often than not the answer is exactly that of the alcoholic or dope addict when asked why he purchased his latest provisions: "I don't know why I did it. I didn't want to do it. I just couldn't help it." The boy knows that in view of the punishment and the likelihood of discovery the satisfaction for which the act was performed does not warrant the risk. It is true that he did not want to lie. Although, therefore, his act is apparently a case of doing what one wants to do rather than a case of doing what one ought to do, such a formulation can be seriously misleading. One could just as well say that it is a case of doing what one has to do rather than doing what one wants to do.

Here, as in the case of the alcoholic, common usage allows either description. The essential difference between the boy and the alcoholic is that the particular desire which prompted the boy had not yet been solidified through habit. Were it to be solidified, it would be entirely indistinguishable from more typical cases of compulsive behavior; and were the world so arranged that pleasures could be as regularly and cheaply obtained through lying as they can through the purchase of a bottle, compulsive lying would be no rarer than compulsive drinking. Perhaps, in fact, it is.

For me, then, conscience is not the voice of a superempirical authority, nor is it the vision of eternal ideas of right and wrong. It is rather the voice of our more basic desires and the abstract awareness of the full consequences of our acts protesting against the claims of more or less compulsive, lower-level desires with their more immediate appeal.

It should be noted that my analysis is not open to the objection that it confuses the pangs of conscience with simple frustration of desire. Frustration denotes the feeling that arises whenever we discover that means-activities which we thought would lead to the fulfillment of desire do not do so, whereas the pangs of conscience exhibit the presence of conflicting desires of specific types. Neither is this analysis open to the objection that it over-intellectualizes our moral life or reduces it to a simple, mechanical calculation of satisfactions. The knowledge required for the moral life on my theory includes not only an abstract awareness of the consequences of our acts as revealed through common-sense observation and the special sciences, but also a concrete, imaginative representation of these consequences as mediated through the entire wealth of personal experience.

It might none the less be said that even if this analysis of the cases cited were correct, this would not establish what it purports to establish, since these cases do not constitute true instances of conflict between desire and conscience; that in the examples given the agents were merely taking a calculated risk; that their mental distress prior to the act expressed no more than doubt as to their chances of success or fear of punishment, whereas their mental distress after the act was an instance of plain frustration rather than of moral regret. Those likely to urge this objection would insist that to be sure that these persons were, in fact, troubled by a bad conscience we should have to know whether they believed in the wrongness of their acts. Only on this condition could we speak of a case of conscience.

This objection has a superficial plausibility. To meet it, the procedure followed up to this point should be made explicit. At the beginning of this section cases of conflict between conscience and desire were characterized in terms of states of indecision, distress, and/or regret accompanying the performance or contemplation of acts that are contrary to rules of behavior to which the agent feels committed or that he believes promote his own interests at the expense of others. In effect, this was my working definition of conflict between conscience and desire. My justification for initially defining a case of conscience in this way without mention of right or wrong is twofold. First, it seems clear that the characteristics cited are alone sufficient to identify all cases of what we ordinarily mean to denote when we speak of conflict between conscience and desire. Second, if I incorporated into my initial definition a mention of right and wrong, I would be courting serious confusion by allowing the intuitionist to beg the very question at issue. The intuitionist says that the cognitive element in cases of conscience is knowledge of right and wrong imparted by a special faculty of the soul. I say that the cognitive element involved is ordinary, empirical knowledge of our more basic desires and the full consequences of our acts. My contention turns on a point of fact, and presumably that of the intuitionist does as well. If, however, the intuitionist means by a wrong act one that is not in accord with the dictates of "conscience," he cannot, without making his contention true by definition, insist that knowledge of the wrongness of an act be required to define a case of conflict between conscience and desire.

It may still be felt, however, that my analysis does not allow a distinction between painful appraisal of self-interest and true moral conflict or that I have failed to explain why one is so strongly tempted to define a case of conscience as a conflict between a belief in what is right and a desire to do what is wrong. The answer to this is as follows. Even on my definition, a conflict between conscience and desire must involve a belief that the act involved is either selfish or contrary to rules of conduct that have elicited our assent. Cases of conscience are thus distinguished from cases of nonmoral calculation of self-interest. If, for instance, a man were distressed and indecisive about the choice of a career or were to regret his decision after having made it, this would not constitute a case of conscience unless he had reason to believe that his choice was either selfish or contrary to some recognized rule of behavior. Since the two most common descriptive characteristics of acts conventionally regarded as wrong, namely, selfishness and opposition to moral rule, are included in my definition, justice is done to our strong feeling that a moral conflict is a conflict between what we believe right and what we desire, without bringing into the picture loaded definitions of the terms "right" and "wrong."

Finally, it may be felt that although my analysis of conscience does permit a differentiation between mere appraisals of self-interest and true cases of conflict between duty and desire, it none the less often robs conscience of its authority where the true long-range interests of the individual bid him violate conventional moral rules. And indeed it does. But since it is almost universally recognized that the deliverances of conscience as traditionally conceived may on occasion be false, this objection is without force. Any adequate moral philosophy must provide a criterion of right and wrong; and although my criterion may not meet with approval, this is irrelevant to the analysis of conscience as a concrete psychological phenomenon.

CONSCIENCE AND SELF-SACRIFICE

So far I have discussed conscience as expressed in a state of bad conscience; I have been concerned to show that what is popularly called a conflict of conscience and desire is, in fact, a conflict between specific types of desires. We must now examine the question of conscience as a positive spur to action, *i.e.*, as a motive for acts of self-sacrifice and benevolence. It is here that we encounter the strongest empirical arguments for conscience as a motivational factor over and above desire, habit, and compulsion. It might be said, for instance: "How can you deny either that desire is self-seeking or that men do sometimes sacrifice their own most basic desires for the sake of helping other persons realize theirs? To take an extreme example, the man who dies to save the life of a comrade in arms is surely not heeding the voice of his more basic desires nor computing the satisfactions and dissatisfactions of the total consequences of his act. He is clearly acting in the interests of others at the expense of his own best interests. The motivation of his act must therefore be totally independent of desire. Whatever prompts him to act in this way is what I call conscience, and however mysterious it may be it is a fact that must be reckoned with and to which no naturalistic account of conscience can do justice. To treat an act of this kind naturalistically is not only to strain the facts but also to deprive it of its moral worth."

The usual naturalistic reaction to this kind of criticism is to deny that desire is always self-seeking. A number of philosophers have pointed out, rightly, that there is no logical impossibility in a man's taking a personal and immediate satisfaction in the contemplation of another's welfare or being frightened or unhappy at the contemplation of another's misfortune. They also point out, rightly, that the immediate spur to action is not the future situation itself but the immediate feel, pleasure or pain, that the envisaged situation produces at the moment of action. Finally, they point out, again rightly, that the anticipated fear of another's misfortune and the desire to avert it, along with the anticipated pleasure of his well-being and the desire to ensure its realization, are not only motive forces that lead to acts of self-sacrifice but also conditions of their moral worth.

This answer, although logically correct, is not quite adequate. It is certainly true that we are not bound by logic to define desire in such a way that one could not be said to desire another's welfare, but it is equally true that in ordinary discourse the term "desire" is frequently used in this narrow sense and that no gross logical blunder is being committed in this case either. The problem is to explain why there is such a strong tendency to define the term so narrowly. The facts are that we have all learned socially acceptable practices through a system of rewards and punishments and that we all regularly check and control our behavior in an attempt to determine what future satisfactions it affords us personally. We easily understand how we learn to promote the interests of others when by doing so we succeed also in promoting our own. We are, however, perplexed and sometimes positively incredulous when it is claimed that our interest in and desire for the welfare of others may become so strong that we stop checking and controlling our actions by reference to personal future satisfactions, as we surely do when we risk even our lives for the sake of others. It is not, therefore, the logical possibility of unselfish or self-sacrificing desires that must be established but rather the psychological mechanism by which they become concrete realities.

Another popular answer is that of Hutcheson and Hume, who postulated the existence of a native or congenital trait that they called the "sentiment of benevolence." There is, however, little or no evidence for the existence of a congenital spirit of benevolence; as I shall try to show in Chapter VI, our specific attitudes toward others seem to develop in the course of experience as a result of specifiable causal factors. Furthermore, unless we wish to resort to the desperate expedient of making a man morally responsible for his native endowments, the theory of natural benevolence does not allow us to praise or blame a man for the performance or nonperformance of acts of self-sacrifice.

On my own theory, morally valuable acts of self-sacrifice are explained as exemplifications of habit-patterns themselves deliberately cultivated for the promotion of self-interest. That this interpretation does not considerably diminish the number of acts of self-sacrifice with moral value will be made apparent in the course of the analysis.

Before turning to this analysis itself, it will be best to examine the term "self-sacrifice." If we use the term broadly to designate any acts that are injurious to the interests of the doer but beneficial to others, then we must distinguish three subclasses. The first is comprised of those acts injurious to the doer though beneficial to others inspired by a simple miscalculation of self-interest. All sides admit that this class of acts is morally valueless. The second class is constituted by cases in which a man promotes the interests of others at the expense of his more obvious self-interests in the conscious expectation of being applauded or otherwise rewarded, as when a man risks his life with the conscious intent of saving the life of a child *and* enjoying the title of hero. The moral value of acts of self-sacrifice in this second class is disputed. The third class includes all those cases in which little, if any, deliberate calculation of self-interest is made, in which a man simply witnesses the distress of others and comes to the rescue despite a clear consciousness of danger to himself, and in which the thought of reward even in the form of self-esteem plays a negligible role. The moral value of this class of acts has rarely been questioned, but the existence of cases answering to this description has been debated. Some theorists, claiming that self-interest is the only possible motivation of human behavior, have tried to analyze all instances of self-sacrifice either as a miscalculation of gross self-interest or as a bid for ego-satisfaction. These attempts are frequently plausible. Even deliberate martyrdom may sometimes be explained in this way: witness T. S. Eliot's subtle analysis in *Murder in the Cathedral* of Thomas à Becket's motivation, where an explanation of this type is left open even at the very end of the play. Often, however, these attempts are indisputably artificial; and as a rule some reference to unconscious self-seeking motives must be invoked to make them at all persuasive. But the resort to the concept of unconscious desires is, in my opinion, a feeble dodge. I, therefore, admit this third class of acts of self-sacrifice without attempting to reduce it either to the first or the second, and it is this class that I most particularly wish to explain.

As stated above, I hold that all morally valuable acts of self-sacrifice are by-products of the rational search for personal well-being. Then how can it be that a man may in a specific case perform a morally valuable act of self-sacrifice in the knowledge that it will not contribute to his total well-being? The answer turns on the expression "in a specific case." Let us lay out the elements of the solution: (1) If a man were to attempt to decide by deliberate and conscious calculation what is in his own best interests every time he is called upon to act, life would soon become an intolerable burden. He therefore allows a great number of his actions to be performed unthinkingly in accordance with once deliberately chosen rules of conduct, which thus become habits—rational or nonrational according to the comprehensiveness and accuracy of the fund of knowledge he used to formulate the original rule of conduct. And, of course, the more habitual a mode of conduct becomes, the less amenable it is to conscious control. This is the price we must pay for efficiency. (2) One of the most valuable rules of conduct is that of attending to the interests of others and promoting these interests as a means to the achievement of one's own personal goals. Unless early childhood experiences are particularly unfavorable, this rule of conduct becomes a deeply entrenched habitual mode of response at a very tender age. Consider, for example, how soon the child learns that many of his wants will be satisfied only if he humors his parents. (3) In view of the close relationship between other persons as means and one's own pleasures or satisfactions as ends and in view of the familiar phenomenon that I shall call "hedonic spread," the happiness or distress of others soon becomes an immediate object of pleasure or pain for ourselves that we naturally strive to produce or to avert.

If we bear these three points in mind, is there still any reason for surprise that a man should spontaneously and without reflection come to the aid of another in distress even at considerable risk to himself? The desire to promote our own selfish interests, our obvious reliance upon the well-being of others as a means, and the universal tendency to feel pleased or pained at the presence or absence of suitable means to our ends fully explain why we should be *disposed* to perform acts of self-sacrifice. That we rely largely upon well-established habits of response for the achievement of our ends fully explains why no conscious process of deliberation need intervene to check the disposition to action. There is no reason, therefore, to postulate "conscience" as a distinct motivational factor, and one can also do without Hume's natural benevolence or instinctive sympathy.

Here again the nonnaturalist would like to interpose an objection: "You have promised to show that your analysis does not rob acts of self-sacrifice of their moral worth. But so far all you have done is show how they are possible, not why they are desirable. And in the course of showing how they are possible, you have made benevolence and self-sacrifice into compulsive habits. You claim that the basic, or fundamental, desire is self-interest, and since you have defined compulsive behavior as desireful behavior that conflicts with or is inappropriate to the realization of fundamental desires, self-sacrifice and benevolence are in a class with alcoholism and drug-addiction. If self-sacrifice and benevolence are morally valuable on your theory, then alcoholism and drug addiction ought to be morally valuable as well. Moreover, you claim to have established a place for reason and conscious deliberation in the moral life, but by your own analysis reason and conscious deliberation become an obstacle to such highly developed moral behavior as self-sacrifice. If all of a man's desires were fully rational and noncompulsive, in your use of these terms, he would be monstrously selfish."

This objection derives its plausibility from several sources. First, there is a failure properly to distinguish between the pursuit of self-interest and selfishness. There is no reason to suppose that the man who consistently pursues his own interests is selfish. A selfish man is simply one who fails to take an immediate, personal satisfaction in the well-being of others. Second, although I believe that men are born selfish and that in the absence of appropriate circumstances remain selfish as adults, I refuse to identify basic desires with originally selfish desires. The view that original desires are also necessarily basic is a gratuitous piece of metaphysical speculation associated with theories of unconscious motivation and traditional self-realization theories that I most vigorously reject. A basic desire is not an original desire or an innate drive waiting to be unfolded. It does not antedate conscious experience; it rather emerges in the course of experience as our knowledge and understanding increase. It is a principle of conduct that we believe would bring us greater over-all satisfaction than any envisaged alternative—a principle, moreover, upon which we do not necessarily always act but upon which we would like to be able consistently to act. Third, and most importantly, this objection rests upon a failure to recognize that man is living in a world in which all of his desires can not be simultaneously realized and that he is capable of knowing this to be the fact. Almost every action is a gamble; every choice, a choice of a lesser evil or a greater good. We must, therefore, choose between, on the one hand, a life in which almost all of the personal pleasures that depend upon the good will of others, as well as the pleasures of love, friendship, and social approbation themselves, are bought at the expense of modes of response that may require self-sacrifice and, on the other hand, a life without this type of risk in which those pleasures and satisfactions are absent. In most cases nothing is nonrational about the choice of the former alternative, and it is unlikely that many persons who represented to themselves the full situation accurately and concretely would fail to choose it.

It is, of course, true that on my account a man who stopped to reflect long enough before coming to the aid of others might check his generous impulses. But then if he pushed his reflections still further he might also come to the conclusion that a life in which such generous habits play no part is not worth living or that such habits entail satisfactions that make the risk worthwhile. Unless the deliberation that led to the formation of these habits was itself nonrational or circumstances had greatly changed since they were formed, this is indeed the most likely outcome. And it is precisely this that distinguishes a noncompulsive from a compulsive habit. It rarely happens that persistent reflection upon his drinking persuades an alcoholic that the satisfactions it affords compensate for the dissatisfactions to which it leads. If this did happen, if the circumstances of the alcoholic's life were such that the lugubrious pleasures of intoxication were the most he could reasonably hope for, then he would not be a compulsive drinker.

In my view, then, the social value of an act of self-sacrifice is proportionate to the strength and the rationality of the habit that it expresses. The strength of the habit is measured largely by the number of times it has been acted upon. Its rationality is measured by its tendency to promote the interests of the agent, due allowance being made for the fact that habits are often unamenable to voluntary control and that individual acts springing from them may on occasion be contrary to the agent's best interests. The second of these criteria, *i.e.,* the rationality of the habit, has been justified by the arguments in Chapter I. The first, the strength of the habit, is a criterion that few will question and that almost all of us actually use in ordinary moral discourse. If, for instance, a man performed an act of self-sacrifice for the first time in his life, we should all suspect him of having miscalculated his interests, whereas if his act of self-sacrifice is one in a long series of similar acts, we do not hesitate to recognize its merit.

My account also has the advantage of explaining why calculated acts of self-sacrifice (the second class of acts in the classification above) are generally regarded as having less moral value than spontaneous ones (the third class). We know that a man who needs the incentive of social approval or some other reward to perform an act of self-sacrifice is less likely to be consistently self-sacrificing and benevolent than the man who does it without this incentive. To go as far as some intuitionists, however, and deny any value to this second class of acts would be extremely dangerous. The pursuit of approval by others is an important element in the development of spontaneous other-regarding virtues. In attributing positive value to acts inspired by this desire we are, therefore, doing more than making a concession to human weakness. We are recognizing the value of a motive but for which the full flowering of human sympathy and compassion would be impossible. This is not, of course, to deny that the desire for social approval may take forms highly repugnant to any developed moral sense. The cold conceit involved in the quest after mere popularity is particularly vicious. Moreover, as I shall argue later, the desire for social approval often conflicts with the desire to follow the dictates of an enlightened conscience and sometimes even masquerades as true conscience. The point here is simply that the desire for approval by others ought not to be held suspect in itself.

Before closing this section we must deal with one last objection. If mature reflection upon the value of other-regarding habits were to reveal that they are unlikely to bring substantial personal reward either in immediate satisfaction or in future well-being, then these habits would be nonrational or compulsive, no matter how desirable they might be from the standpoint of society. One can well imagine that the person interested in justifying the ways of God to man, as well as the old-fashioned moralist with his insistence upon absolute and inviolable moral rules, will be disturbed by this feature of my theory. Granting, however, that this is not the best of all possible worlds, what possible motive is there for denying that there are moral casualties; and granting that one of our primary moral obligations is to make this world into a better one, why should we wish to dispense with this wholesome reminder that personal morality is rooted in the social order and presupposes a substantial measure of social justice? In fact, this aspect of my analysis is only an extension of what Hume put so well in the eighteenth century and what was illustrated so dramatically in Europe during and immediately after the war: when the scarcity of human goods becomes acute, rational justification for adherence to conventional moral rules is impossible.

We must face the tragic fact that we are not living in a world in which private and immediate social interests always coincide and that only in such a world would other-regarding virtues invariably bring their personal reward. Until such a time arrives, habits of benevolence will not always be perfectly adapted to serve our basic and fundamental desires, and there will necessarily be men whom the social order excludes from the moral order. But in facing such facts our gain is greater than our loss, for only in this way are we likely to overcome complacency with respect to social injustice. Nor need we fear that a widespread acceptance of these obvious facts will necessarily usher in an age of social chaos and disregard for established moral values. The thesis that self-sacrifice without reward is irrational is in no way incompatible with the thesis that happiness without self-sacrifice is illusory. The thesis that social justice is a condition of personal morality is in no way incompatible with the thesis that personal morality is a condition of social justice. The thesis that this is a tragic and imperfect world is in no way incompatible with the thesis that it is a perfectible one. But as long as we insist upon the present reality of a perfect moral and social order, what reason have we to devote our energies to the creation of a better one?

chapter three

THE DEFINITION OF GOOD

I contend that there are no serious moral problems that cannot in principle be resolved by the practice of rationality. This contention rests in part upon the belief that the concept of moral good can be defined in much the same way that indisputable empirical concepts such as light or color may be defined. This belief, which is that of most traditional moral philosophers, has met with considerable skepticism in the twentieth century. Contemporary philosophers who accept, as all but a few do, a formal definition of right conduct as conduct that promotes the good have not usually denied that the concept of right conduct may be dealt with empirically. If, for instance, one declares that the moral good is identical with social well-being and that right conduct is conduct that promotes social well-being, then the problem of deciding what concrete conduct is right not only can but must be resolved by purely empirical methods. Many contemporary philosophers have, however, argued either that the concept of the good is not definable at all or else that any proposed definition of the good must be radically different in kind from definitions of empirical concepts. An examination of these arguments will help further to clarify my own position.

THE ALLEGED INDEFINABILITY OF GOOD

The most famous argument designed to establish the indefinability of good is that of the English philosopher G. E. Moore, whose *Principia Ethica* of 1903 has been highly influential in determining the direction that moral philosophy has taken in the Anglo-American world ever since. Although Moore is an intuitionist, he is not an intuitionist of the kind discussed in Chapters I and II; he does not believe that one can intuit the truth of statements with respect to our moral obligations or duties. On the contrary, he insists, as I do, that statements about moral obligations must be supported by empirical propositions showing that the performance of these obligations leads to the good. The disagreement turns on the possibility of defining good or justifying statements about the good by recourse to empirical propositions.

According to Moore, statements about the good are assertions that something possesses a simple, unique, unanalyzable, and nonnatural or nonempirical quality. This unique quality is the proper denotation of the word "good," and the truth of statements asserting that an object or a class of objects has this property can be established only by intuition. When, therefore, we ask whether anything is good, we are asking whether we can intuit that this thing does in fact possess the nonnatural property of goodness. And when we ask whether pleasure is good, we are asking whether we can intuit that all or most things having the property denoted by the term "pleasantness" also have the unique, nonnatural property denoted by the term "good."

Since, according to Moore, "everybody is constantly aware of this [notion of goodness],"[1] the possibility of anyone's making a mistake with respect to these questions arises from the fact that "he may never have become aware at all that it [the notion of goodness] is different from others of which he is also aware." In other words, the quality of goodness may be so intimately related to some other quality, such as pleasantness, that we fail to recognize that they are distinct and thus mistakenly call an object good when it is only pleasant or mistakenly assume that statements such as "Pleasure is good" are definitions rather than statements about what is the case:

[1] All quotations from G. E. Moore will be found in his *Principia Ethica* (Cambridge: The University Press, 1954), Preface and ch. 1.

> . . . it is very easy to conclude that what seems to be a universal ethical principle is in fact an identical proposition; that, if, for example, whatever is called "good" seems to be pleasant, the proposition "Pleasure is the good" does not assert a connection between two different notions but involves only one, that of pleasure, which is easily recognized as a distinct entity.

To this mistake Moore gave the name "naturalistic fallacy," and by pointing it out he hoped that nobody would ever again attempt to "foist upon us such an axiom as that 'Pleasure is the only good' or 'The good is the desired' on the pretence that this is 'the very meaning of the word.' " To the philosophers who allegedly made this mistake, Moore gave the name "naturalists."

Moore claims that all definitions belong to one of three categories. First there is what he calls "the verbal definition proper" —what most philosophers today call reportive, or lexical, definitions. These definitions are merely reports, such as one finds in a dictionary, of the way in which people do as a matter of fact use certain words. Second, there is what Moore calls "the arbitrary verbal definition"—what most philosophers today call stipulative definitions. These are statements announcing the intention of the speaker to use a word in a certain way. When one coins a term and states how one shall be using it, one is giving a stipulative definition. Third, there are definitions that enumerate the parts of a complex whole. Here it is best to allow Moore to speak for himself. He says,

> You can give a definition of a horse, because a horse has many different properties and qualities, all of which you can enumerate. But when you have enumerated them all, when you have reduced a horse to its simplest terms, then you can no longer define those terms. They are simply something which you think of or perceive, and to anyone who can not think of or perceive them, you can never, by any definition, make their nature known. And so it is with all objects not previously known, which we are able to define: they are all complex; all composed of parts, which may themselves, in the first instance, be capable of similar definition, but which must in the end be reducible to simplest parts, which can no longer be defined.

Now, Moore has no difficulty showing that alleged definitions of the good cannot be seriously intended as purely reportive definitions or pure stipulations. He says, rightly, that when a moral philosopher makes a statement such as "Pleasure is the good" he cannot seriously intend merely to state how the word "good" is ordinarily used. "Nor do I think that any exponent of naturalistic ethics would be willing to allow that this was all he meant. They are all so anxious to persuade us that what they call the good is what we really ought to do." Assuming, however, that they were proposing their definitions of good as mere reports on common usage, "how perfectly absurd is the reason they would give for it. 'You are to do this, because most people use a certain word to denote conduct such as this.'" Similar considerations make it equally clear that the moral philosopher is not merely announcing his *intention* to use the term "good" in a certain way. Nobody is so naïve as to suppose that his bare decision to use the term "good" in a certain way constitutes an adequate reason for behaving in a certain way.

If, therefore,

> it is not the case that "good" denotes something simple and indefinable, only two alternatives are possible; either it is a complex, a given whole, about the correct analysis of which there may be disagreement; or else it means nothing at all, and there is no such subject as ethics. . . . Neither of these possibilities has, however, been clearly conceived and seriously maintained, as such, by those who presume to define "good"; and both may be dismissed by a simple appeal to facts.

To this first argument Moore adds two others. One of these has since become known as "the open-question argument." If, says Moore, statements of the form "X is good" (where X stands for anything whosoever, be it pleasure, the greatest happiness of the greatest number, the direction of historical or evolutionary process, eternal bliss, the maximum satisfaction of individual interests, or what have you) were genuine definitions, then these statements would be linguistic trivialities, whatever term X stands for and "good" being strictly interchangeable. Questions of the form "Is

X really good?" would become insignificant. If, to take an example, "Pleasure is good" were a definition, then the question "Is pleasure good?" would be equivalent in meaning to "Is pleasure pleasant?" or "Is good good?" But, Moore says, "whoever will attentively consider with himself what is actually before his mind when he asks the question 'Is pleasure (or whatever it may be) after all good?' can easily satisfy himself that he is not merely wondering whether pleasure is pleasant."

The third argument gives more direct support for Moore's contention that "good" stands for a simple, undefinable, nonnatural quality. If, he says, anyone tries the "mental experiment" of attending to what is present to his mind when he asks of each suggested definition of good whether it is really what he means by good, he

> may become expert enough to recognize that in every case he has before his mind a unique object with regard to the connection of which with any other object a distinct question may be asked. Everyone does in fact understand the question "Is this good?" . . . Whenever he thinks of "intrinsic value" or "intrinsic worth" or says that a thing "ought to exist," he has before his mind the unique object—the unique property of things—which I mean by "good."

The first of these three arguments will be dealt with in a later section. For the moment suffice it to say that Moore has failed to recognize a perfectly legitimate type of definition that is very common in the natural sciences and to which we shall later assimilate definitions of the good.

The second argument can be disposed of with the simple remark that there is no reason to assume that every definition is a pure triviality. Most definitions in the natural sciences, especially the controversial ones, are proved not to be trivialities by Moore's own criterion, since we can meaningfully ask, as scientists constantly do, whether these definitions are satisfactory. There can be no question, for instance, that at one time scientists did actually define heat in terms of phlogiston, and it is only on the assumption that scientists did not regard this definition as a pure triviality that we can account for its finally being abandoned.

The third argument, like all arguments of the same type, is more difficult to refute. There seems to be no way in which one can prove in any strict sense of the term that someone does not intuit what he claims to intuit. But there are several considerations that might cause us to hesitate before accepting Moore's claim to intuit a simple, nonnatural property of goodness. One of these is that this power of intuiting a simple, nonnatural property of goodness appears not to exist in most persons. And this objection is really much stronger than it appears at first sight, since Moore claimed that we all do have this property present to mind whenever we ask "Is X really good?" and it is difficult to believe that so many persons are ignorant of what they actually have present to mind.

A second difficulty can be explained as follows. Suppose Jones says that White is a good man and Black a bad man. Suppose further that Jones complies with a request to give as complete a description as possible of both White and Black, naming every empirically observable property of both. Finally, suppose that the two descriptions are identical in every respect, both men being equally honest, equally kind, equally idealistic, etc. We then ask Jones why he says that White is a good man and Black a bad man. He answers: "Because I intuit that White has the unique, nonnatural property of goodness whereas Black does not." Jones' answer is, of course, fantastic; no one would be satisfied with it. Yet, if what we meant in saying that X is good is that X possesses a unique, nonnatural property that can only be intuited, it is difficult to see why this answer seems so strange. To meet this objection an intuitionist might argue, and some have, that the nonnatural property of goodness is regularly associated with certain empirical properties in such a way that anything that has this nonnatural property also has one or more of these associated empirical properties. But in this case judgments of goodness and badness can be adequately founded upon a knowledge of the empirical properties of that about which these judgments are made rather than upon controversial intuitions. No practical purpose would be served by invoking intuition.

A third consideration turns on the fact that the intuitionists are not in a favorable position to discuss moral issues successfully, even with one another. Assume that one intuitionist intuits that X is good and a second intuits that X is bad. If both of them claim infallibility for their intuitions, all either can do is accuse the other of moral blindness or willful perversity. If they do not claim infallibility for their intuitions, they can hardly do more than look again and urge the other to do the same. At most, they might offer one another a few tips on how to cultivate their intuitive powers. Those who argue that the intuited property of X is somehow associated with other, natural properties of X are in a somewhat more favorable position here than those who do not. They might say that if one attends long enough to the associated properties which can be empirically observed and publicly discussed, one will finally intuit the presence of the nonnatural property of goodness itself. But again either the presence of these associated properties is sufficient to justify the judgment or it is not. If it is, talk of nonnatural properties is superfluous. If it is not, there is a residuum of intuitive awareness necessary to resolve the issue, and no amount of public discussion or empirical observation will be of avail. I repeat that neither this nor the two foregoing considerations prove that Moore's position is false. They are introduced chiefly to indicate how unfortunate it would be if his position were true and thus to dispose the reader to look for a happier solution.

One final point. Of Moore's three arguments the open-question argument has been historically the most significant. As has already been seen, this argument fails because it falsely presupposes that definitions must be linguistic trivialities. The argument does, however, have the virtue of pointing out that the word "good," unlike a word such as "bachelor," is not in ordinary usage associated with any one set of criteria that everybody is prepared to accept as essential or definitive. For X to be a bachelor, it suffices that he be a man and that he not be married; these criteria are universally recognized, and they are the only recognized criteria. Linguistic considerations alone, therefore, govern our usage of this term, and it is this that renders its definition so uninteresting and uninformative to anybody who knows the

English language. The criteria by which we identify X as good are, however, more numerous, less universally recognized, and much more complexly related to one another. For these reasons any clear definition of good, any selection of certain criteria as defining, or essential, traits, will depend upon more than an analysis of ordinary usage or purely linguistic considerations, and it is precisely this that accounts for the non-trivial character of definitions of the good.

I do not mean to suggest that my own implicit definition of moral good in terms of personal well-being and social welfare involves any great departure from ordinary usage or that in choosing these two traits as definitive I have not been guided in large part by linguistic considerations. On the contrary, I am convinced that both in ordinary discourse and in philosophical literature one discovers considerable reluctance to use the term "good" to denote what is not an element in both personal well-being and social welfare. And were this not the case, I should not be so bold as to adopt the position I have adopted. Moreover, my disagreement with the Kantians, who tend to define moral good almost exclusively in terms of adherence to rule, can, I believe, be resolved by a simple appeal to ordinary usage. Very few persons would be willing to say that adherence to a moral rule when this is contrary to the best interests of society is an instance of the good. And Kant himself, though he formally defined the good in terms of adherence to rule, implicitly appealed to the criterion of self-interest. He was so convinced of the "inappropriateness" of a state of affairs in which virtue would not be rewarded with personal happiness that he "postulated" a system of rewards and punishments after death; and in several passages he adopted the Platonic tactic of celebrating the satisfactions involved in adherence to moral rule, declaring them not only superior, but incomparably superior, to the satisfactions of "mere" desire fulfillment.

Extralinguistic considerations *are* required, however, to settle the disagreement between myself and strict utilitarians, whose definition of the good exclusively in terms of social welfare is the major alternative to my definition and because of whose influence the criterion of social well-being has come today to weigh more heavily in our minds when we think of moral behavior than the criterion of self-interest. For, if the utilitarians hesitate to accept my definition, it is because they believe that the criterion of self-interest is often incompatible with the criterion of social welfare—and this is a question of nonlinguistic fact. If it were agreed that these two criteria are not incompatible, the utilitarian would not only have no solid reason for objecting to my definition but would almost certainly welcome it. There are three reasons for this. (1) Long-established usage recognizes a class of largely self-regarding virtues, *e.g.*, temperance and prudence, to which a strictly utilitarian definition of the good does not give due prominence. (2) As Moore rightly pointed out, definitions of the good are not usually considered adequate unless they have a bearing on our conduct, unless they offer at least implicitly a good reason for behaving in a certain way. And, it is to be presumed, the greater their bearing on conduct, the better. If, therefore, behavior that promotes the social good also promotes private good, it would be highly desirable to incorporate reference to private good in our definition and thus formally enlist one of the most powerful of human motives on behalf of the moral enterprise. (3) A strictly utilitarian definition of the good has moral and political implications that offend the sensibilities of everyone who believes in the worth or sanctity of the concrete, living individual. Most human beings are, in fact, offended by demands that the individual sacrifice his ultimate well-being for the sake of the community. This is not simply because they suspect hypocrisy or sham here but also because they believe on moral grounds in the individual's right to the pursuit of happiness.

"PERSUASIVE" DEFINITIONS OF GOOD

A number of moral philosophers, especially those known as emotivists, have attacked the naturalists, not by arguing for the indefinability of the good, but rather by arguing that definitions of the good (and, indeed of all moral concepts) are totally different in kind from definitions of empirical concepts. These emotivist philosophers normally construct their argument from the premise that moral statements are used to express attitudes of favor or disfavor. (That moral statements *do* normally express attitudes of favor or disfavor can be readily seen from the fact that the person who said "X is morally good, but I do not approve of it" would be almost certainly accused of abusing the English language. In ordinary English usage, one rarely says that something is morally good unless one has an attitude of approval toward it.) From this premise it follows that, given any proposed definition of the good, it should be the case that what is said to be good elicits a favorable attitude on the part of the definer. But since this condition need not be met by definitions in the natural sciences, definitions of the good and definitions of indisputably empirical concepts are alleged to be radically different from one another. To secure general agreement about the proper definition of an empirical concept, it suffices to secure general agreement with respect to rules of linguistic usage and to the relevant facts—something that we can hope to achieve by purely rational methods. To secure general agreement on the definition of the good, however, it is necessary to secure general agreement in relevant attitudes—and this we cannot reasonably hope to do by rational methods alone. To mark the difference between the kind of definition involved in ethics and other types of definition, it has become customary to refer to moral definitions as "persuasive definitions."

One well-known emotivist, A. J. Ayer, expressed his skepticism about the possibility of securing general agreement on moral issues in the following terms. "Argument," he says,

> is possible on moral questions only if some system of values is presupposed. If our opponent concurs with us in expressing moral disapproval of all actions of a given type *t,* then we may get him to condemn a particular action A, by bringing forward arguments to show that A is of type *t*. For the question whether A does or does not belong to that type is a plain question of fact. . . . What we

> do not and cannot argue about is the validity of these moral principles.[2]

At this level we are dealing with what Ayer calls "pure questions of value,"[3] and our pronouncements with respect to these questions have as their source *pure* feelings or attitudes, by which Ayer apparently means feelings or attitudes that are not causally conditioned by beliefs and cannot be altered by changing beliefs.

Ayer's conviction that pure feelings underlie our higher-order moral judgments derives in part from linguistic considerations of the type outlined in the brief initial statement of emotivism above. But it also derives from a belief that many of our feelings on basic moral issues are products of brute social conditioning. Having explained that we often cite facts to resolve moral disagreements in the expectation that agreement on the facts will lead to the adoption of similar moral attitudes, Ayer goes on to say:

> And as the people with whom we argue have generally received the same moral education as ourselves, and live in the same social order, our expectation is usually justified. But if our opponent happens to have undergone a different process of moral "conditioning" from ourselves, so that, even when he acknowledges all the facts, he still disagrees with us about the moral value of the actions under discussion, then we abandon the attempt to convince him by argument. . . . It is because argument fails us when we come to deal with pure questions of value, as distinct from questions of fact, that we finally resort to mere abuse.[4]

Unfortunately, Ayer forgot to press the meaning of such terms as "moral education" and "social conditioning." Had he done so, he would probably have seen the necessity of resorting to some other theory about the origin of our moral attitudes to uphold their "purity." Ayer, like many others, has overlooked the extent to which social and moral conditioning proceeds by way of indoctrination in belief. If, for instance, one holds that birth con-

[2] A. J. Ayer, *Language, Truth and Logic,* 2nd ed. (New York: Dover Publications, Inc., 1946), pp. 111–12.
[3] *Ibid.,* p. 11.
[4] *Ibid.,* p. 111.

trol ought not to be practiced, this may well be the result of social conditioning. But it is a form of social conditioning that has proceeded almost wholly by way of indoctrination in beliefs: that there is a God, that the hierarchy of the Church is competent to interpret God's will, that men will be punished in an afterlife for contravening his commandments, etc. Individual attitudes toward a certain class of acts may also be affected by the bare impact of emotively charged terms when these are habitually employed in a given society to evaluate this class of acts. But this method of conditioning rarely, if ever, occurs without a simultaneous indoctrination in belief. Furthermore, even if this method were used more or less independently, the attitude so produced would still be contaminated by beliefs, since the efficacy of the method is almost always tied to a belief of the conditioned individual in the wisdom, benevolence, or power of the conditioners. If we wished to alter an attitude so conditioned, it might very well be sufficient to convince the individual that certain of his factual beliefs with respect to his moral authorities are false.

The skepticism of Charles Stevenson, who is probably the best known of all emotivist philosophers, is less radical than that of Ayer. Stevenson explicitly recognizes that much disagreement in attitude is "rooted in" disagreement in belief in the sense that "the former can be reconciled by reconciling the latter." He says even that he is prepared to entertain the hypothesis that "all disagreement in attitude is rooted in disagreement in belief" and possibly to adopt it as a "heuristic principle." None the less there is a substantial strain of skepticism in his *Ethics and Language*. Almost in the same breath in which he suggests the adoption as a heuristic principle of the hypothesis that all disagreement in attitude is rooted in disagreement in belief, Stevenson instructs us to treat this hypothesis with "scientific caution" since "we have learned how problematical any psychological generalization, even when it is less sweeping than this one, must inevitably be. . . . It is even possible that increased knowledge would be hostile to ethical agreement."[5]

[5] Charles Stevenson, *Ethics and Language* (New Haven: Yale University Press, 1944), pp. 136–37.

The sources of Stevenson's skepticism are not very different from those of Ayer. He says,

> People with different racial or temperamental characteristics, or from different generations, or from widely separated communities, are likely to disagree more sharply on ethical matters than on factual ones. This is easily accounted for if ethics involves disagreement in attitude; for *different temperaments, social needs, and group pressures would more directly and urgently lead these people to have opposed attitudes than it would lead them to have opposed factual beliefs.*[6]

But what reason is there for believing that different social needs and group pressures influence attitudes to a greater extent than they influence beliefs? Social needs and group pressures do, for example, help considerably to explain anti-Semitic attitudes in Nazi Germany, but the beliefs about the Jews then current in Nazi Germany were no less distinctive than the attitudes with which they are associated and can be traced to the same source. Stevenson has probably been misled here because he failed to distinguish between beliefs that are relevant to the resolution of moral issues and beliefs that are not; for, although it is probably true that different social groups may come more readily to agree on factual beliefs that do not bear on moral feelings or attitudes, it seems quite clear that agreement on factual beliefs that do engage moral sentiments is neither easier nor more difficult to secure than agreement on the moral issues themselves.

As for temperamental factors, what reason is there for believing that they have any bearing at all upon moral attitudes or beliefs? Is there, for instance, any evidence that men with strong homosexual leanings tend to evaluate homosexuality differently from the general run of mankind? It may be that the relative incidence of condemnation and tolerance among the nonhomosexual population is the same as the relative incidence of self-condemnation and self-acceptance among the homosexual population. And even if there were a significant difference between the attitudes of homosexuals and those of heterosexuals, would we have to ex-

6 *Ibid.*, p. 18. Italics mine.

plain this difference as a direct consequence of temperamental peculiarities? Perhaps we would be closer to the mark in saying that the homosexual's urgent personal interest in the problem forces him to give the matter fuller consideration than others and thus to substitute rational judgment for popular prejudice. Finally, even if there were a significant difference between the attitudes of homosexuals and those of heterosexuals and even if this difference were correctly attributed to temperamental bias, would it follow that the attitudes due originally to temperamental bias were not functions of belief in that they could not be altered by changing belief? Surely, many persons have learned to compensate for temperamental bias; to show that a belief is due to temperamental bias rather than to rational examination of the issues is almost automatically to undermine that belief.

Stevenson's own example of a moral disagreement that "*seems* [italics his] rooted in temperamental differences" is a disagreement on the question of free love between an "oversexed, emotionally independent adolescent" and an "undersexed, emotionally dependent adolescent."[7] I am not quite certain what Stevenson has in mind by emotional dependence or independence, but it does not seem to me that a difference in strength of the sexual urge is a barrier to rational agreement on the question of free love. Presumably, Stevenson means to suggest that the undersexed adolescent will suffer relatively less from a policy of sexual abstinence and will consequently be less inclined to favor free love. But why should the undersexed adolescent, if he is minimally rational, not see that abstinence is harder on others than on himself and take this into account in deciding what his attitude will be toward free love? And why should the oversexed adolescent not recognize his own temperamental bias? And why, if he recognizes it, should he not allow his views to be determined accordingly? Although it is reasonable to suppose that strongly sexed persons are more likely to engage in premarital or extramarital intercourse than weakly sexed persons, it does not seem to me that they are therefore likely to adopt a more relaxed view with respect to the moral merits of such intercourse. The opposite

[7] *Ibid.*, pp. 136–37.

might even be the case. Certainly, it is doubtful whether St. Augustine's uncompromising opposition to free love ought to be explained as a result of his having been weakly sexed.

The skepticism of these philosophers about defining moral terms by rational methods thus derives from two sources. One is the unfounded belief that differing moral attitudes have their source in brute social conditioning or native temperamental peculiarities so deeply rooted that they cannot be altered by rational methods. The other source is the set of linguistic considerations outlined at the beginning of this section and to which I shall now return.

Now it is clear that a definition of the good would be persuasive in that one would not choose a denotation for the word "good" unless one approved of it. It is also clear that definitions in the recognized empirical sciences are not persuasive in this sense. If one defines heat in terms of kinetic energy, it could not reasonably be inferred that one approves of kinetic energy; whereas if one defines the good in terms of the full exercise of one's native capacities, it can be reasonably inferred that one approves of exercising one's native faculties. This difference between definitions in the natural sciences and definitions in ethics will be willingly granted. Does it follow, however, that definitions in ethics are *essentially* or *radically* different from definitions in the recognized empirical sciences? More specifically, does it correctly follow that in the recognized empirical sciences, as opposed to ethics, prior agreement in attitude is unnecessary to secure agreement with respect to the definition of key concepts? Most emphatically not! This conclusion follows only from the wholly fallacious premise that if the definition of purely empirical terms does not depend upon attitudes of favor or disfavor *toward what the term finally denotes,* it does not depend upon attitudes of favor or disfavor of any kind whatsoever, but only upon linguistic considerations and factual beliefs.

Consider a few examples. If the definition of a whale as a certain kind of mammal is generally agreed upon, this is certainly due in part to the fact that whales have been observed to share certain anatomical properties with other mammals and to linguistic conventions regarding the use of the term "mammal." But it is also due to the fact that the person who accepts this definition has a desire for a system of zoological classification that permits him to systematize as much existing knowledge about animal species as possible. The person who had no such desire, who was interested only in securing a classification of animal species that would permit him to make inferences with respect to their natural habitats, would prefer a definition of whales as fish. Similarly, if a definition of heat in terms of kinetic energy or color in terms of light waves is generally agreed upon, this is due in part to the correlation observed to exist between felt heat and sensed color, on the one hand, and to the behavior of molecules in motion or light waves, on the other, plus linguistic conventions governing the usage of the terms involved. But it is also due to the fact that persons who accept these definitions have a strong desire to explain natural phenomena in mathematically precise language. The person who has no such desire will not be willing to accept them. Finally, to take a third example, if ever physicists come to an agreement on a definition of light, they will do it not only because of new factual discoveries or new linguistic conventions but also because they have a common interest in explaining as many phenomena as possible, in as mathematically precise a theory as possible, and with as little departure from highly confirmed existing theories as possible. In the absence of this common interest or desire, there would be little or no hope for eventual agreement on a definition of light. The point that these examples illustrate is that definitions are usually designed to serve a purpose and that unless there is agreement on the purpose there is little likelihood of agreement on the definition.

Of course, the kinds of underlying desires or attitudes that permit such agreement as exists on definitions in the recognized empirical sciences are different from the kinds of underlying desires or attitudes that permit such agreement as exists on moral terms. The practical desires that establish agreement in scientific inquiries are of the kinds just mentioned and, ultimately, the desire to predict and to control the future course of events. The desires that establish agreement in moral inquiry—the desires that permit, for instance, nearly universal agreement that acute and widespread suffering must be excluded from any definition of ultimate good—are the desires for individual and social well-being. But it cannot be argued, as we have just seen, that agreement in attitude is not equally necessary to the successful resolution of disputes with regard to definitions in the recognized sciences as well as in ethics.

Moreover, it cannot even be argued that the desires that give impetus to scientific inquiry are more universal than the desires that give impetus to moral inquiry. Surely, men are as universally interested in personal happiness and social harmony as they are in the prediction and control of their environment. In fact, common sense clearly indicates that the individual's desire to predict and control the natural environment is largely subsidiary to his desire for personal fulfillment and social well-being; and if one pursues this thought, it soon becomes apparent that in a very real sense science is a branch of ethics, as Peirce and some other pragmatists contended. Neither can it be successfully maintained that the desires that underlie scientific inquiry are somehow more rational than the desires underlying moral inquiry. In the ultimate, root sense of the term the rationality of any desire has to be judged in terms of its aptitude to promote well-being; and one would be throughly unjustified in suggesting that the desire for well-being is itself less rational than the desire for prediction and control.

If one wishes at all costs to make invidious comparisons between the possibility of defining moral and purely scientific terms, the only line of attack left is that moral concepts are more vague and thus practically—though not theoretically—more difficult to define than scientific ones. But even this distinction of degree tends to evaporate if, instead of focusing one's attention upon textbook paradigm cases of scientific definitions, one reviews the whole body of scientific concepts. Certainly sociological and psychological concepts such as mental health, maturity, the unconscious, perceptual gestalts, topological space, anomy, and hundreds of others are no less vague than the concepts one discovers in the literature of moral philosophy. And if we examine the less-developed natural sciences or controversial concepts employed even in the highly developed natural sciences, we will not be disappointed in a search for vagueness and ambiguity.

MORAL CONFLICT AND CONFLICT OF INTEREST

Another line of attack on the possibility of securing general agreement on moral issues by rational methods emerges very naturally from the emotivist frame of reference. Since the empirical, or scientific, method is a publicly acceptable technique for determining the truth or falsity, and thereby securing the uniformity, of beliefs, it would seem to follow that if conflicting moral attitudes on any given issue were functions of beliefs, as the "naturalist" believes to be the case, there would necessarily be a publicly acceptable technique for securing agreement in moral attitudes. It has been argued, however, that this inference is invalid. Suppose that Jones believes an envisaged situation would substantially satisfy his desires, whereas Smith believes the same situation would substantially frustrate his desires. Suppose further that Jones and Smith each share the other's belief. Would we not here have agreement in belief and disagreement in attitude? And how can one reasonably expect that disagreement in attitude under these circumstances could be resolved by rational methods?

In answer to this line of argument, several comments are in order.

1. Cases of the kind described do frequently occur; and although in ordinary language we refer to them more simply as conflicts of interest, they could also be called without gross confusion instances of agreement in belief and disagreement in attitude. But they are not necessarily instances of agreement in belief and disagreement in *moral* attitude. Conflict of interest per se is not moral conflict. Football players on opposing teams have con-

flicting interests and so do competing businessmen. But in neither case would we be justified in regarding the conflict in itself as a case of moral disagreement. Moral disagreements do regularly express conflicts of attitude, but conflicts of attitude do not necessarily manifest moral disagreement.

2. One of the primary goals of the moral enterprise is to mitigate and where possible totally eliminate painful conflicts of interest by securing adherence to appropriate general rules of conduct. To use the truism that conflicts of interest actually exist as evidence for the impossibility of resolving moral disagreements by rational methods is, therefore, wholly indefensible. It is very much as if one were to say that we cannot mitigate or eliminate existing conflicts of interest because we have not yet done so.

3. It is, of course, true that many persons tend, often strongly and with different degrees of awareness of what they are doing, to rationalize their own selfish interests, arguing for the social utility of modes of conduct that are in fact socially pernicious. But rational procedures are not only in principle competent to expose moral rationalizations of this kind; they are the only conceivable means by which this job can be done.

4. Finally, it is also true that many persons, though recognizing the social value of some given moral rule, do not always live up to it. But the failure of an individual to live up to a moral rule does not invalidate the moral enterprise any more than the failure of a scientist to live up to the ideals of objectivity prescribed by his profession invalidates the scientific enterprise. The failure of an individual to live up to a moral rule whose general adoption would be socially desirable proves nothing but the need for rational efforts to enlist support for the rule. If observance of the rule in question is in the ultimate interests of the individual, he must be made to recognize this, and his habits of rational self-control must be strengthened to the point where he can act accordingly. If observance of the rule is not in his best interests, then sanctions that make it in his best interest must be instituted. In either case, we can appeal to rational procedures. "Mere abuse" is far from being our only recourse, as Ayer and apparently Stevenson believe.

If I am not mistaken, Ayer and Stevenson are in an important sense victims of the absolutist tradition that they are trying to undermine. Having recognized that one cannot rationally justify adherence to established moral rules under all circumstances and having seen the futility of mere moralizing, they conclude that morality is bankrupt. What they do not see is that this conclusion follows only from the conservative premises of the tradition against which they are arguing, most especially the view that the task of the moral philosopher is to demonstrate the universal validity of conventional moral rules; for, when morality is viewed from my standpoint, *i.e.,* as part of an attempt to create a more perfect and harmonious social order, the demise of absolutism and merely hortatory ethics is not a sign of bankruptcy but rather an opportunity to gain a hearing for an ethics that is more pertinent to the problems of contemporary life.

chapter four

RATIONALITY AND THE PURSUIT OF TRUTH

My principal arguments for the view that rational pursuit of self-interest ought to be encouraged by the use of moral sanctions were presented in Chapter I. Those arguments, it will be recalled, were as follows: (1) In a reasonably well-ordered society most socially undesirable behavior is not in the best interests of the individual agent himself and would automatically disappear if the individual were *rationally* to pursue his best interests. (2) In cases where socially undesirable behavior is in the best interests of the individual, it would usually be easier to eliminate future behavior of this sort by a revision of social institutions than by the use of moral censure; not only because moral censure is at best a relatively weak motivating force in cases of this kind but also because it is likely to embitter the agent and thereby reinforce antisocial tendencies. (3) By openly declaring that an individual has no moral obligation to act counter to his best interests and by actively working toward the elimination of social circumstances that lead him to violate the conventional moral code, we would create a social climate that disposes the individual to cooperate with, rather than to defy, the community.

The first of these arguments presupposes that the individual could promote his best interests by the practice of rationality; the second and third rest heavily upon the assumptions that the practice of rationality can lead to social betterment and that it is in the interests of almost all persons to contribute to social betterment. In this and the following chapter, I shall attempt to defend these largely commonsensical assumptions. First, I shall offer a definition of rationality.

DEFINITION OF RATIONALITY

The term "rationality" is here used to stand for a variety of practices, which it will be convenient to group under six headings.

1. Before deciding on matters of any moment, the rational man will seek out whatever relevant data he believes it practically possible to uncover without undue difficulty. The qualifiers "practically possible" and "without undue difficulty" will often render the application of this criterion somewhat difficult. But their necessity is readily apparent. Where the issue at hand is complex and great advantages are to be gained by quick decision or where the issue is one of relatively little moment, the loss of time and effort involved in collecting all the data that one believes to be relevant and available may often count for more than the loss to be expected from deferring a decision, even though the decision is mistaken. Vagueness notwithstanding, the criterion is serviceable, especially where someone willfully refuses to conform to it because he suspects that a knowledge of the facts will oblige him to opt for an alternative he is initially inclined to envisage with distaste. Consider, for instance, the person who refuses to consult a doctor because he fears an operation will be recommended; the military commander who refuses to listen to his advisers or the would-be musician who refuses to take a test of musical aptitude for fear that this would mean an end to his ambitions; or the bigot who reads only those newspapers and journals that reflect his political or religious views for fear that he may have to surrender comfortable prejudices.

2. Both in the collection of data and in the drawing of implications from this data, the rational man will employ the generally accepted principles of inference. No one, of course, will be sur-

prised to find logicality listed as one element of rationality, but it should be noted at once that logicality is merely one element among six and an element to which no more nor less importance is attached than to any of the other five. That the present criterion does not surpass in importance the first can be seen from the famous case of the logical madman, whose madness consists not in his inability to reason but in his inability or unwillingness to face facts. Rationality is not only a more inclusive concept than logicality; it is also a concept of vaster human significance. And I cannot too strongly protest against those who tend to run the two ideas together to score a cheap victory against rationality. Unfortunately this procedure is as common as it is dangerous.

3. The rational man will make great efforts to discover and to protect himself against those innate or acquired dispositions and habits of thought that warp his judgment. Some of these, such as the tendency to accept without sufficient critical evaluation views widely held by the social groups to which one belongs and to believe nothing but good of those whom one loves, are nearly universal. Others, such as are most dramatically illustrated by the emotionally disturbed, have their source in one's personal history or temperamental bias. The paranoiac who sees an attack in every word and gesture of others is an example. It should not be forgotten, however, that periods of national hysteria or professional preoccupations may produce similar tendencies among so-called normal men—tendencies even more dangerous because they are more insidious and less easy to detect.

4. The practice of rationality requires that one frequently submit one's views to the criticism of others. Strictly speaking, this criterion is not independent of the first three. It may, in fact, best be regarded as a means of satisfying the criteria already mentioned, since the value of submitting one's views to the critical evaluation of others consists precisely in that it is largely through others that we add to our stock of useful information, detect our errors of inference, and discover our biases. This criterion is often difficult to apply. It would be idle to submit our views to the criticism of persons from whom we can expect no help. At times it is not practicable to do so. On other occasions the decisions that

follow from our convictions are so trifling that discussion would be a waste of time. Only a knowledge of the concrete situation can help us to determine whether we are justified in ignoring this criterion and relying wholly upon our own resources. None the less, neither the fact that this rule admits of exceptions nor the fact that it is often difficult to determine in specific cases whether an exception is legitimate invalidates the rule. The man who does not defend his views against intelligent and informed critics can, if he is rational, repose only a very limited confidence in them. The believer in free enterprise and Western political institutions who refuses debate with serious critics has even less right to his convictions than the citizen of a strictly authoritarian society who has no opportunity of defending his convictions against others has to his.

5. The rational man will remain open-minded with respect to all of those issues that do not warrant firm conviction. And if he has conscientiously sought the truth by the methods indicated in criteria (1) through (4), he will be under no illusion as to the width of the domain within which firm convictions have no place. In matters of knowledge, certainty is the ideal to which we aspire, but probability is the reality with which we must come to terms. Although this criterion is almost universally honored in principle, it is much less often honored in practice. Men are so impatient with the labor of reflection and so anxious for certainties that they normally terminate an inquiry no matter how ill founded the conclusions it yields, provided only that the conclusions reached appear for the moment more plausible than their contradictories. Moreover, men find it all too easy to persuade themselves that the exigencies of practical affairs or the necessity of resolute action obliges them to set doubts aside. We forget that our concern is with the future as well as with the present and that the surest way of depriving ourselves of the knowledge that the future alone can bring is to repose an excessive confidence in the evidence presently available.

6. The five criteria that precede are alike in that they are concerned with the discovery of truth. But to be rational, it is not enough to pursue the truth. Although usually our acts do con-

form to our convictions, cases in which they do not are by no means rare and in such cases we often invoke the term "nonrational." A man may, for instance, have reviewed the facts, drawn the logical conclusions, protected himself against personal biases, sought out the advice of competent advisers, and come to the conclusion that he can easily succeed in an enterprise of great importance to himself without, however, being able to take the initial steps. His failure to act on his conviction is clearly nonrational. Consider a second, more concrete example. A man at the gaming table may have calculated his chances of winning by making a given move and convinced himself that his chances are almost nil. Yet he makes the move. Here, too, we would often speak of nonrationality. To what extent we may succeed in conforming our behavior to our convictions is a question that will occupy us in the sequel. For the moment suffice it to say that the rational man must attempt to give his convictions the weight and efficacy of living beliefs.

Although the above definition of rationality is intended to correspond in the main to ordinary usage and may, if I am not mistaken, be rightly regarded as an explication of the meaning of that term as employed in everyday language, the reader who feels that it does not accord with accepted usage is asked to regard it as a stipulative definition. My concern is less to explicate the meaning of the concept than to defend the value of the practices enumerated.

I should also like to emphasize that the concept of the rational man as here defined is distinct from that of the intelligent man or the well-educated man. It would, of course, be most surprising if the thoroughly rational man did not make a fuller use of his intellectual powers and were not better informed than a less rational man. Conversely, it would be most surprising if highly intelligent and well-informed men did not find the practice of rationality more natural than others. None the less, rationality is less an achievement or a state of being than a set of dispositions —dispositions that even a relatively unintelligent, ignorant, and unpracticed man may display. The willingness to seek out whatever data is available before deciding on practical matters, to discover one's biases, to submit one's opinions to critical examination by others, and to keep one's mind open on issues that do not warrant firm conviction, as well as the readiness to act on one's firm convictions, are obviously moral dispositions rather than intellectual attainments. The element in rationality that demands the most in the way of intelligence is the second, that requiring the employ of generally accepted rules of inference. But even here the moral, as opposed to the intellectual, factor is of the utmost importance; since the failure of logicality in practical matters is far more often the result of willful disregard of generally accepted rules of inference than of inability to employ them.

Finally, I should like to point out that my definition involves no opposition, or antithesis, between rationality and feeling, or affectivity. The function of rationality is not to banish feeling or passion, but to guide and direct them. I do not disparage the disinterested desire for knowledge that has been largely responsible for the development of modern science nor persons with mathematical-logical minds who prefer to deal with highly abstract but precise concepts such as constitute the working materials in the more developed natural sciences. But rationality is no less closely allied to practical wisdom than to scientific intelligence. Its working materials are the vague but practically indispensable concepts of ethics and the social studies. And this is as it must be since rational inquiry is inspired by the desire to resolve urgent personal and social problems, and its goal will not be achieved until those problems, in which we have a great emotional investment, have been resolved.

RATIONALITY AND INFERENTIAL KNOWLEDGE

Although the pursuit of truth is an important part of rationality, it is by no means the whole. This is evident, not only because rationality requires us to act upon the truth as well as to search after it, but also because it is meaningful to ask whether the pursuit of truth is itself fully rational. The root sense of rationality, that which normally commands and determines our concrete descriptions, is, as I mentioned in the last chapter, the adaptation of means to ends. He who employs means appropriate to the achievement of desired goals is acting rationally; he who fails to do so is acting nonrationally. This means that to defend a specific definition of rationality is primarily to show that the practice of rationality so defined is a crucial means to the achievement of human wants. This does not mean, however, that one can dissociate the notion of rationality from that of pursuit after truth. The thinker who believes that the search for knowledge is inimical to human well-being is invariably taxed with the title of irrationalist. If, therefore, my primary task is to defend my conception of rationality by showing its usefulness in achieving basic human values, I am none the less confronted with the secondary task of showing that the practices I have designated by the term "rationality" do lead to the discovery of truth.

First, however, it should be observed that in saying that the practices enumerated above lead to the discovery of truth I am saying both too little and too much. Too little because it is necessary to show not only that these practices lead to the discovery of truth but that they constitute the only generally reliable means for the discovery of truth. Too much for two reasons. One is that it is not necessary to show that rationality can lead to the discovery of the truth with respect to any and every issue that arouses our curiosity but only with respect to those issues that have a bearing upon practical conduct. The second is that it is not necessary to show that rationality will lead to the truth with respect to every practical problem. It is enough that rationality demonstrate its value by producing probable evidence sufficient to guide conduct in a large number of cases.

One very common attack upon rationality has been summarily and somewhat inexactly expressed in the phrase "I believe because it is absurd"—a phrase attributed to the early Church father Tertullian. This attack has many versions of varying degrees of sophistication, but all are alike in that they call into question the value of inferential knowledge. One concrete example goes as follows. It is impossible to conceive that God should be incarnated as a man, since God is by definition superhuman. However, since God loves man, since he can best show his love by an act of incarnation, and since he is omnipotent, it is reasonable to believe in incarnation. That we find the doctrine absurd must, therefore, be due to a limitation of the human understanding. This limitation cannot be overcome, and it will be a constant source of doubt. However, the doctrine being reasonable on other grounds, the doubts that we experience with respect to it should be set aside.

The fallacy in this argument lies in the supposition that if two or more propositions of which we are equally persuaded lead to logically contradictory conclusions, this must be taken as evidence of a limitation of the human understanding. Why should it not be taken as evidence that at least one of the original beliefs is false? Of course, if one could incontrovertibly establish the truth of the several premises considered individually as well as the validity of our deductions, the soundness of the argument would have to be admitted. But it is precisely this possibility that I am calling into question. If it is admitted, not only the rules of logic but even the conditions of intelligible discourse go by the board. For the argument establishes far more than its authors usually intend—namely, the nonapplicability of the principle of contradiction.

It is noteworthy that arguments of this general type are resorted to only in defense of beliefs to which their authors are passionately committed. In mundane affairs these persons rely, like everybody else, upon the ordinary rules of logic, and they are no less annoyed than the rest of us by a second party's violation of these rules. It is also noteworthy that these persons seldom allow their opponents the same liberties in defending their passionate convictions that they arrogate to themselves.

Another and even more famous instance of this line of reasoning has been proposed by Kant, who like Tertullian was eager to "deny knowledge in order to make room for faith." According to Kant, by a process of rigorous deduction from incontrovertible premises one is sometimes led to draw two mutually incompatible conclusions. One can, for instance, prove both that the world does and that the world does not have a beginning in time. But were Kant's premises as incontrovertible as he thought they were? Were his deductions as rigorously logical as he believed? If they were, why have most competent philosophers remained unconvinced? And what must one think about a logical demonstration of the illogicality of logic? If one invokes the established principles of logical inference to prove their incompetence, one is involved in a vicious circle. If, on the other hand, one attempts to demonstrate the incompetence of the ordinary principles of deductive logic by an appeal to a different set of principles, how can one guarantee the validity of this allegedly superior logic?

This defense of knowledge acquired by logical inference is not intended in any way to disparage knowledge based on experience —the kind of knowledge that the ordinary man of affairs would put to the account of "good judgment" or that some feminists might believe to derive from a "womanly intuition." It was already pointed out that logicality is only one element among six in the complex of practices we call rationality. The influence of classical rationalism, which attributed inordinate importance to the inferential operations of the mind and in which knowledge was almost entirely identified with the products of such operations, is much to be regretted. So limited a conception of reason and knowledge could not fail to produce the type of distinction that Pascal expressed in opposing *l'esprit géométrique* to *l'esprit de finesse,* that Newman expressed in opposing notional knowledge to real knowledge, that inspires the ordinary man when he urges us to beware of reason and to put our trust in impulses born of experience, and of which the conservative avails himself when he inveighs against the intellectual and asks us to repose our faith in the accumulated wisdom of the ages.

Knowledge based largely on memory and practical experience is no less genuine than the knowledge of the geometer or the physicist and no less important in the practical affairs of mankind. Without it we could perform few of the tasks of daily living, and we would be hopelessly lost whenever a crisis in human relationships developed. But if it is a mistake to disparage or to neglect good judgment and intuitive knowledge, it is no less a mistake to ignore the background of reflection needed to produce it. The person whose intuitions are quickest and most reliable is indeed a person with experience of the world, but he is also a person whose intuitions are least blind. Just as of two scientists working on the same problem the one who has reflected on the problem the most and who knows the most about it in the narrow scientific sense is the more likely to intuit the solution, so of two persons placed in the same milieu the one who has in the past made the fullest use of his inferential powers is the more likely to come to an accurate intuitive appraisal of the problems encountered. And just as the scientific genius must test his intuitions by experimental methods, so the practical man will learn to submit his intuitions to the test of discursive elaboration. Logicality is only one among six elements in rationality, but it is no less necessary than the others.

RATIONALITY AND OPEN-MINDEDNESS

A second and very popular argument against rationality as I have defined it calls into question the criterion requiring open-mindedness where evidence is inadequate or where arguments on one side of the issue are counterbalanced by equally solid arguments on the other side. William James in his famous essay "The Will to Believe" used this argument. It runs somewhat as follows. It frequently happens that our belief with respect to a given proposition is itself a factor determining both the truth of that proposition and our future well-being; and if in such cases there is no positive evidence indicating the falsehood of this proposition, then we ought to believe it. To illustrate with one of James's examples: If a man hopes to succeed in marrying the woman he loves and if there is no evidence to indicate that this is impossible, then he has everything to gain and nothing to lose by believing in his success, since that belief may well be a factor determining the outcome of his efforts; thus the belief makes the proposition true.

The weakness in this argument springs from a double confusion. In the first place, James failed to distinguish between two meanings of the word "belief." To mark this distinction sharply, it will be advisable to introduce a terminological convention. The state of mind that follows upon a process of deliberation during which evidence for and against a given proposition is critically examined and an inference made as to where the weight of evidence lies will be called a conviction. The man at the gaming table who having calculated mathematically the possibility of winning by making a given move and having found that it is slight or nil will be said to have a *conviction* that he will lose. If the man acts upon this conviction by refraining from making the move, he will also be said to have *pragmatic belief* that he will lose, pragmatic belief being characterized as a disposition to act. Although it is obvious, as we have already seen, that men frequently have convictions without appropriate pragmatic belief, the two do normally go together and many philosophers have gotten into serious confusion, as did James here, by failing to distinguish between them.

In the second place, James failed to distinguish between the proposition *that it is in our best interests to act as if a proposition might be true* and the proposition *that the proposition is true.* This distinction is of the utmost importance because pragmatic belief in the first of these propositions does not, whereas pragmatic belief in the latter obviously does, exclude serious attempts to confirm or to disconfirm the proposition in the light of later developments.

With these distinctions in mind, let us ask what exactly James could have meant in his argument on behalf of the will to believe? Obviously, he could not have meant that the man in the example given ought to convince himself that the woman he loves will marry him. By hypothesis he has no evidence that she will and by definition one cannot be convinced of the truth of a proposition unless one does have evidence for it. Neither could James have meant that the man ought to induce a state of pragmatic belief appropriate to the conviction that the woman will marry him, since the man has no conviction that she will. The only thing James could reasonably have meant is that the man ought to act as if the woman might marry him, which is in effect to encourage pragmatic belief in the proposition that it is in his best interests to act as if the woman might marry him. But on the assumption that the woman in question likes vigorous and forceful men, pragmatic belief in the latter proposition implies an attempt to overwhelm her by his entreaties, and there is nothing at all nonrational about this course of action.

Unfortunately James's confusions led him to betray his true intent and to give the impression that one does at times have the right to convince oneself of the truth of a proposition in the absence of evidence. That this would be an unwise policy can, however, be seen concretely by reference to James's own example. If, for instance, the man were convinced that the woman would say "yes," what would be the point of his trying to overwhelm her with his entreaties and win her by force? It is only on the supposition that the proposition "she will marry me" might be false that this action makes any sense. And worse, if the man allowed himself a firm conviction that the woman will marry him in the absence of evidence, then he has eliminated a condition for the acquisition of fuller knowledge when more evidence becomes available. Finally, since a state of conviction follows upon an appraisal of relevant evidence, the only available nonrational method for cultivating a state of conviction with respect to any issue is that of deliberately ignoring relevant considerations. And this is a policy that James surely did not wish to recommend.

The difficulties to which a failure to observe these last few points may lead are nicely illustrated in one contemporary philosopher's treatment of the problem of faith. He rejects flatly the existentialist view according to which "the essential significance of religious faith lies in the belief in the absurd," saying, as I would, that anyone "deludes himself if he persuades himself that he believes a contradiction which he knows to be a contradiction." He adds, however, that faith does not

> merely adjust the strength of its attachment to an idea to the degree of rational probability attached to it. It adjusts its attachment to the *value* of the idea, and the rational probability of the idea is accepted as one phase of its value. In some situations, e.g., in faith in a bank's solvency, the element of rational probability is the most important consideration in the estimate of value. In other cases, such as faith in the innocence of a friend accused of a crime, the objective evidence is of much less significance in determining the estimate of value by which the attitude of loyalty, or faith, may be justified.[1]

If my analysis is correct, two mistakes are made here. (1) It is as impossible to be convinced of a proposition, knowing that evidence is lacking or insufficient, as it is to be convinced of a proposition that one knows to be self-contradictory. (2) There is a confusion between acting toward a friend accused of a crime as if he might be innocent and convincing oneself of his innocence, for loyalty to a friend accused of a crime does not require conviction with respect to his innocence. Loyalty to a friend requires only that one be prepared to help him and to act in his interests whatever the facts of the case may be. When this is carefully borne in mind, it can easily be seen why one should not allow friendly feelings to obscure one's judgment. It is only too obvious that this might make it more difficult to help the friend. If it turned out that he was guilty after all, one would be totally unprepared.

There is still another set of problems connected with the Jamesian doctrine of the will to believe that requires examination. So far, I have distinguished between conviction and pragmatic belief; there is, however, still a third meaning of the term "belief." Consider again the example of the man at the gaming table. Let us assume that this man is convinced that a given move will fail. It could well be that despite this conviction his imagination runs away with him. He easily pictures that the move will be successful: he "feels" or "sees" the number seven, for example,

[1] A. C. Garnett, *Religion and the Moral Life* (New York: The Ronald Press Company, 1955), p. 124.

coming up. Now, this greater readiness to envisage one state of affairs rather than a contrary one—something that happens not infrequently even when one is convinced that some contrary state of affairs is more likely—will here be called emotive-pictorial belief. When a man acts contrary to his convictions, this is usually because of the presence of an inappropriate emotive-pictorial belief—emotive-pictorial belief being much more intimately related to pragmatic belief than to conviction. It would, however, be as unwise to confuse emotive-pictorial belief with pragmatic belief as it would be to confuse it with conviction. For emotive-pictorial belief does not always give rise to action. The man in our example, for instance, might very well act on his conviction in spite of his emotive-pictorial belief.

Now, with respect to emotive-pictorial belief two questions arise. One is: Ought we ever to allow or encourage this kind of belief when it is inappropriate to conviction? To this question the answer is affirmative. Consider the following cases, both of which were posed, though in slightly different ways, by William James. A man's life depends upon his ability to jump across a narrow mountain gorge. Although by any rational estimate he is more likely to fail than to succeed, it would obviously be advantageous for him if he were to believe in his success. A man has good, but not conclusive, rational grounds for suspecting that an associate will act toward him in a hostile manner. By dwelling upon this possibility he is likely to provoke the behavior feared; whereas by cultivating an emotive-pictorial belief in the other's good intentions he may be able to avert the anticipated behavior. Here again, it could well be advantageous for the man to cultivate an emotive-pictorial belief at odds with rationally warranted conviction.

These and similar cases, however, have two important aspects that are all too often overlooked by those who point to them in order to deprecate rationality. First, these cases constitute exceptions to general rules. When our life depends upon the successful performance of a certain feat, it is wise to encourage emotive-pictorial belief in our ability to do it. But in general, it is most unwise to exaggerate the extent of our abilities, since this misrepresentation will often prevent us from actually cultivating them. Similarly, when the good will of an associate depends upon the attitudes we display in his company, it is a good idea to cultivate attitudes that will evoke his good will, especially while we are in his company. But it would be most unwise consistently to overestimate the good will of others, since consistent misrepresentation of other persons' good will leads to disillusionment. In other words, there are *exceptional occasions* when we ought to cultive emotive-pictorial beliefs that contradict rationally warranted conviction, but we ought never to make it a *general policy* to cultivate such beliefs. Second, it is by the use of rational procedures as defined above that we must decide when exceptions are warranted. We would not, for instance, cultivate emotive-pictorial belief in our ability to jump across the gorge without first being satisfied that this is the best chance. An initial overconfidence in our abilities would be dangerous in that it would discourage the search for other and safer solutions. Similarly, we ought not to cultivate an emotive-pictorial belief in the good will of an associate unless we have first rationally satisfied ourselves that we thereby stand a good chance of disposing him favorably toward us. If we have not done this, we are likely to be victims of an unscrupulous maneuver.

The second question that arises with respect to emotive-pictorial belief is: Ought we ever to allow or encourage these beliefs in the absence of any conviction for or against the reality of the state of affairs envisaged? To this question the answer is again affirmative. But, as before, this affirmative answer does not have the irrationalistic implications that might be supposed. Let us assume, for example, that a man has in the present no means of forming a rational conviction about the ultimate nature of the universe. None the less, temperament or circumstance leads him to adopt a vision of the universe as a warm and friendly place that supports his deepest aspirations or else as an indifferent medley of blind physical forces that thwart his deepest longings and against which he must pit his will. Now, if the notion of rationality is allied strictly with the notion of truth, there would be nothing nonrational about the adoption of either of these pictures of the universe, provided only that the man did not mistake his emotive-pictorial belief for conviction, thereby inhibiting himself from seeking out evidence bearing upon the truth or falsity of his belief as that evidence becomes available. If, however, reason is interpreted as a faculty by which we secure human well-being (and this is its deepest meaning), reason retains its full authority; for a decision to allow or cultivate either of these pictures of the universe will not be rational unless the individual has made a rational appraisal of the consequences to which this decision will lead.

KNOWLEDGE AND MOTIVATION

A third and far more radical challenge to rationality comes from those who argue that knowledge (or reason) does not have the power to influence conduct. One argument of this kind starts from the unobjectionable premise that knowledge by itself does not move us to act. For instance, we do not normally act upon knowledge relating to the chemical composition of heavenly bodies. Knowledge ordinarily moves us to act only if it engages our feelings, only if it is knowledge relevant to the accomplishment of some actually desired goal. From this premise, however, it is falsely inferred that the *original* and *primary* motivation of human behavior is a set of native desires. Knowledge thus becomes merely a "slave of passion."[2] If it should happen that knowledge bids us act contrary to our native desires or passionate commitments, its commands will go unheeded.

Two fallacious beliefs are involved in this argument. One consists in the assumption that knowledge and passion (or knowledge and desire) are two distinct entities. The other consists in the assumption that if knowledge does not move us to act by itself, then passion must be the original or primary cause of behavior. The falsity of the first assumption is evident from the impossibility of defining desire without including in that definition a

[2] The phrase is Hume's, but it is doubtful whether the argument stated here can be correctly attributed to him without qualification.

number of cognitive elements. There is no desire at all unless there is a belief that the goal desired is attainable and that the goal if attained will provide satisfaction to the agent. That cognitive elements are essential ingredients in any desire is also evident from the qualification of desires as either rational or nonrational. If one desires a goal, believing mistakenly either that the goal is attainable, that the achievement of the goal will provide satisfaction, or that there are no dissatisfactions involved such as to offset the anticipated satisfaction, we do not hesitate to refer to the desire as nonrational. If, on the other hand, these convictions are present and we regard them as true, we ordinarily qualify the desire as rational. Like most other motivational complexes that produce human behavior, desires contain both cognitive and affective, or feeling, elements.

The falsity of the second assumption, *viz.,* that if reason does not move us to act by itself, then passion must be the original or primary cause of behavior, can be shown with almost as little ceremony. It is, of course, true that human beings act before they have knowledge, and no doubt this behavior has a cause. But the cause is not passion or desire. If, for instance, it is true that a newborn child naturally seeks the mother's breast, this is not because he has a passion or desire for the mother's milk. The act is purely instinctive. To explain this act as a result of passion or desire one would have to assume that the child knew in advance the satisfaction it would bring. The most that can be said here is that for passions or desires to develop, human beings must be so constituted that they are capable of discovering which experiences bring satisfactions and which, dissatisfactions; but it remains the case that the affective state, the anticipatory feeling of pleasure, peculiar to desire or passion is invariably accompanied by a cognitive state. Neither of these states antedates the other, and neither is less essential than the other. One cannot therefore argue that desires are incapable of being modified as a result of increased knowledge on the grounds that passion or desire is a more original or more primary cause of human behavior.

Another argument designed to show the powerlessness of reason over human conduct takes its cue from the phenomenon of compulsion. This argument is very similar to the last. Because it sometimes happens that knowledge of what constitutes our best interests does not move us to act appropriately, the conclusion is drawn that knowledge cannot ever be the cause of our behavior, that the true cause of our behavior must always be passion. And this argument is inadequate for much the same reason as the last. The inference rests upon the tacit premise that *either* knowledge *or* passion is the cause of conduct, whereas there is no sharp dichotomy. Feeling states move us to act only in cooperation with cognition. Cognitive elements are built into the very fabric of desire. Most compulsive behavior must be attributed either to the influence of habit or to a failure of imagination, *i.e.,* an inability to represent to oneself concretely the full consequences of one's actions. And although the existence of compulsive behavior *is* proof of a limitation of reason, it is certainly not a proof of so radical a limitation as the position I am arguing against suggests. The ability fully and concretely to imagine the consequence of one's behavior can certainly be cultivated by the practice of rationality, and habits that prevent us from acting in accord with our best interests more often than not testify to a prior misuse of reason rather than to any inherent or ultimate weakness in reason. It is largely for this reason that moralists have so insistently demanded that society assume its responsibility properly to educate its members from their youngest years on.

RATIONALITY AND RATIONALIZATION

A fourth and still more radical challenge to rationality comes from those who refer contemptuously and indiscriminately to the products of deliberation as mere rationalizations. Now, the view that all products of deliberation are rationalizations can easily be seen to be untenable. The mere fact that we use the term "rationalization" in a pejorative sense is the tribute that passion pays to reason. If there were no reasonably adequate criteria for distinguishing between a reasoned conviction and a rationalization, between valid and invalid arguments, between correct and incorrect judgments of relevance, there would be as much justice in the claim that all convictions are rational as in the contention that all convictions are rationalizations. The commission of logical fallacies and the distortion of evidence could never have been recognized unless the light of reason had exposed them for what they were. This extreme view, however, has rarely been held.

The more common view is that man is so constituted by nature that the proper functioning of his rational capacities depends upon factors wholly or almost wholly beyond human control either individually or collectively. Now before turning to an examination of these arguments, let it be noted that I am not questioning that rationalizations are in fact widespread. In practical affairs they are far more common than reasoned beliefs. The issue is whether the prevalence of rationalization is due to the very nature of the human personality or whether it is due, as I believe, to social circumstances and imperfect rational discipline on the part of individuals.

One argument is that passions or desires invariably becloud the intellect. This argument is related to and suffers from much the same defects as the argument that desires are primary and original motivations of human behavior, but it is not wholly identical with the latter. The premise is that in practical matters feeling or passion is what initiates and guides inquiry, from which it is inferred that feeling or passion will not tolerate an outcome disagreeable to it. This argument owes its plausibility to a number of confusions.

First, it is true that we do not ordinarily initiate inquiries unless we are interested in the outcome, and it is also true that the interest that initiates and guides many inquiries is that of proving the truth of a proposition that one wishes to be true at the outset. But it is rare for an inquiry to be initiated by a single interest. Most inquiries are initiated and guided by two or more conflicting interests or desires. For instance, a man might have a strong inclination to pursue two professions while knowing full well that he cannot undertake both. In this case it would certainly be fair to ask which initial interest or desire will prevail. The point here is that most inquiry is much more complicated than the argument presupposes.

Second, even though an interest initiates and guides inquiry, it does not follow that the interest will determine the inquiry's outcome. If the preceding discussion relative to the nature of desire is correct, it is as likely that inquiry will modify the initial desire as that the initial desire will determine the outcome. A desire, as we have seen, is a complex of convictions and feelings, and if inquiry shows any of the original convictions to be false—something that frequently happens—then the desire itself will automatically be modified.

Third, the argument begs the question in tacitly presupposing that the desire to know the truth about an issue even though the truth is uncomfortable cannot be a genuine desire capable of competing with other interests. But it should be clear that many men do desire to know the truth for its own sake and that if society were to institute appropriate sanctions this desire could be immeasurably strengthened.

Another argument is that the outcome of inquiry is determined by unconscious factors largely beyond human control. Now it will be readily agreed that factors of which the individual is unaware or insufficiently aware do often determine his beliefs, and it is possible that these factors are more numerous than was generally believed fifty years ago. Few persons are sufficiently aware of the extent to which the desires for social approval and material advantage influence their judgment. And it may be that such things as toilet training or infantile hostility toward the father also have an effect upon later thinking. What I do not grant is that these factors are as difficult to detect or as unamenable to rational control as is generally believed today. My conviction is that the average person who makes a serious effort to detect and counteract these influences can expect at least moderate success, especially if the social environment is favorable.

Let us suppose that at an early age a child had a strong desire to kill his father, that now as an adult he is unaware of any hostility, past or present, and that he vigorously supports religious and political positions of which he knows his father disapproves. It may be that one of the causes of his advancing arguments against his father's views is the hostility that he once felt for his father. On this question I will offer no opinion. But what follows? In particular are we justified in drawing any radically pessimistic conclusions about the efficacy of rational procedures?

Either the man's arguments are sound, or they are unsound. If they are sound, they cannot be called rationalizations, and there is no reason to believe that the infantile hostility actually warped the man's powers of reason. On the contrary, it might be that the hostility the man once experienced toward his father was a factor leading him to the discovery of valid religious and political views. The wish to harm another, whether conscious or unconscious, will lead to a distortion of reasoning only if it is not compensated for by a stronger wish to know the truth. If, on the other hand, the arguments are not sound, there are still no grounds for pessimistic conclusions about the powers of reason. The arguments may not be sound because the man is ignorant of relevant facts or made errors in reasoning. If so, we give him the necessary information or point out his errors. Or else the arguments are not sound because hostility toward his father did actually paralyze or distort his powers of reasoning. In this second case we may attempt either to break down the hostility or to build up the man's desire for the truth so that this motive may be made effectively to compete with the desire to hurt his father. Of course, the resources at our disposal for counteracting influences known to distort judgment often prove inadequate, either because of the tenacity of these influences or because we lack the skill to reinforce motives that can neutralize their effects. But here, as in the case of compulsions, failure is probably due to the agent's or others' neglect of rational procedures at an earlier stage.

In view of the thoroughly commonsensical character of the foregoing considerations it would be natural for the reader to ask whether the widespread tendency to minimize the power of rational practices of which I spoke earlier actually exists. If it does, he might further ask what its sources are.

One source of the tendency that I deplore lies in the Christian-Augustinian doctrine that the proper functioning of human reason depends upon an upright will, which is itself a gift of divine grace. If our nature is vicious, our reasoning is but rationalization and deception. If, however, we are touched by the hand of God, our reason will be illuminated by the light of truth. According to this doctrine, everything is decided in the inmost recesses of the human soul, where the individual becomes one—literally or metaphorically—with the divine nature. I do not claim, of course, that this metaphysical-theological doctrine is very seriously held today by many—not even by Christian theologians. But I do claim that profound and unanalytical suspicion of reason survives the demise of this doctrine. And I do claim that, though the doctrine itself in its original version has for all practical purposes lost its hold over our imagination, its legacy is a strong predisposition toward the romantic notion that the human personality has unsuspected depths difficult to characterize in rational terms but crucial to an understanding of merely "surface" behavior.

I most especially deplore the current enthusiasm for the notion of *the unconscious,* conceived as a mysterious and largely inaccessible dimension of the human psyche comparable to the submerged portion of an iceberg. I do not, of course, mean to pass judgment on the psychoanalytic movement itself, many of whose members treat the notion of the unconscious as a psychic entity with as much suspicion as I do. Nor do I mean to deny that many facts of human behavior are as yet unexplained and that in this sense we are often unaware or unconscious of the motives of our behavior. I do mean to condemn the uncritical use of the term "the unconscious." There are obvious logical difficulties involved in the notion of a consciousness that is not conscious; and although these difficulties in themselves do not necessarily rob the concept of its utility in special contexts, they are sufficient to alert us to the dangers that glib and thoughtless recourse to this idea engenders. For most persons the term itself, quite apart from any theoretical edifice of which it may be a part, suggests something incomprehensible to the normal rational understanding. And once the popular mind has seized or had forced upon it the idea that the unconscious is *the* clue to human behavior, it is almost inevitable that the popular mind will also come to the conclusion that human behavior is either totally inexplicable or explicable only with the aid of esoteric and highly specialized knowledge, thus calling into question the evidence of intelligent common sense and abusing it with epithets such as superficial.

To compensate fully for the nefarious influence of the concept of the unconscious it would be necessary to show that the observable phenomena that have given rise to it could be adequately explained without postulating the existence of an entity corresponding to that notion. And although a comprehensive effort of this kind clearly falls outside the scope of this book, I should like briefly to indicate, without any pretension to thoroughness, how this might be done with respect to the more limited notion of repressed unconscious desires. My contention is that the observable phenomena from which the existence of repressed unconcious desires are normally inferred require for their understanding nothing more recondite than the familiar concepts of false or inadequate knowledge.

It is well known that the psychoanalyst considers a repressed desire as an originally conscious desire of which the agent is ashamed or that has been frustrated during the course of experience. It is also well known that the psychoanalyst is dealing with the behavior of disturbed persons. The contrast between normal and disturbed persons in their reactions to the presence of such desires should, therefore, give us a clue to the use of the term "repressed desire." When a normal person experiences frustrated desire or feels shame because of a desire, the desire is automatically modified or simply drops out of his experience. He will probably remember on later occasions that he once desired this particular goal, and he may even wish that it were still possible for him to attain it. But he is not unduly disturbed and can easily give up of this desire, because he has the capacity to take up other, satisfying goals. In the case of a disturbed person, however, this kind of experience leads to different types of behavior and different types of future conscious states; and our reasons for saying that a person is motivated by a repressed desire all relate to the fact that these latter modes of behavior and conscious states are agreed to be undesirable. The agent cannot easily recall the formerly conscious desire; he feels that life has lost its meaning; he compulsively pursues irrational goals; he cannot bear criticism from others; etc.

There is no reason to suppose that the once conscious desire now continues to exist unchanged in some secret compartment of the mind. And, in any case, the practical problem is not to discover some esoteric technique for peering into this secret compartment of the mind where the formerly conscious desire is now supposedly hidden. The practical problem is to discover (1) why that particular frustration or experience of shame led to this particular type of future behavior and conscious experience and (2) in what way this type of behavior and conscious experience may be controlled and modified. The answer to the first question is in principle quite simple, although, of course, in any particular case a fully satisfactory account may be very difficult to come by. Experiences of this kind lead to unwanted types of behavior and modes of consciousness because the agent's fund of knowledge and experience of life are not rich enough to ensure easy transition to other pursuits. The solution to the second of these problems is no more difficult in principle. The patient's abnormal behavior is controlled and modified by the application of techniques for effecting recall of his now forgotten experiences and/or forcing him to relive in the present crucial experiences of a similar type. The agent must once again, as an adult with an adult's richer fund of knowledge and experience, face the facts that he was unable or unwilling to face as a child, and from a realistic facing of these facts with his richer store of knowledge and experience he must go on to more desirable modes of behavior. The notion of repressed unconscious desire is, therefore, dispensable. We can fully account for the behavior of the person said to be under the influence of a repressed desire by reference to the notions of ignorance or false belief.

chapter five

RATIONALITY AND HUMAN WELL-BEING

The primary purpose of this and the preceding chapter is to show that the practice of rationality is the principal means to the achievement of human well-being, the argument being that the practice of rationality leads to the accumulation of knowledge, which in turn leads to the realization of basic human needs and desires. The two parts of the argument cannot be kept rigidly separate, but in the last chapter the accent fell heavily upon the contention that rationality leads to the accumulation of knowledge. Here emphasis will fall upon the view that knowledge leads to the fulfillment of human aspirations.

That rationality leads to knowledge and that knowledge leads to human well-being are, it should be pointed out immediately, both points of view that can be held only with qualifications. No one today claims that the practice of rationality always and necessarily leads to the acquisition of desired knowledge. Nor does anyone today claim either that knowledge is the *only* condition of well-being or that it *guarantees* well-being. The question is one of degree, my contention being that rationality is the crucial factor among others—crucial in the sense that most other factors promoting human well-being have rationality as their condition and that of the many factors promoting human well-being rationality is usually the easiest to cultivate. As is most often the case where a question of degree is being discussed, argument will for the most part consist in an attempt to expose false beliefs that dispose us to exaggerate.

HUMAN WELL-BEING DEFINED

It has sometimes been maintained that any attempt to define individual good will necessarily fail. Since individuals indisputably differ from one another in many significant ways, the good of one person will differ from the good of another; a satisfactory definition of individual good that holds true for all individuals is therefore impossible.

This argument fails for two related reasons. In the first place, although it is true that human beings differ from one another in many significant respects, it is no less true that they resemble one another in many significant respects. Certain human needs and desires are common to all men or to such an overwhelming majority of persons that for most practical purposes they may properly be counted as universal. In the second place, it is necessary to distinguish between general definitions of individual good, on the one hand, and detailed descriptions of the good for each and every individual, on the other. Of course, the latter are far more concrete than the former, and if they were available, general definitions of individual good would for most purposes be unnecessary. But from this it does not follow, as those who propose the objection under discussion apparently assume, that general, abstract definitions of individual good are either impossible or useless.

General definitions of individual good are *possible* if at the appropriate level of abstraction the distinction between the good of the single individual and the good of the generality of individuals becomes irrelevant. And this is frequently the case: for example, the food required to satisfy the needs of a Mexican peasant is not the same as that required to satisfy the needs of an upper-class Frenchman; food, however, is a universal human need. Definitions of individual good are *useful* if they serve the purpose for which they are intended. Now my purpose here is to provide a definition of human well-being that permits us to determine the role that knowledge plays in promoting it, and there is no valid a priori reason for assuming that a definition useful for this purpose cannot be constructed simply because it is less concrete than might be desired for some other purpose.

A somewhat similar objection is to the effect that any definition of personal well-being will be intolerably vague. Granting the possibility of cataloguing universal and fundamental human needs or desires, how are we to determine how many of them must be fulfilled in order to ensure well-being or the extent to which they must be satisfied? To this objection the answer is that there is no practical need for precision of this kind. If we know what goals are worthy of pursuit and if we know the means of advancing toward these goals, we know as much as we need to know. "Well-being," like "progress," is a relative term. To ask how many desirable changes must be made if there is to be progress is like asking how much progress is progress. Similarly, to ask how many or to what degree basic needs or desires must be satisfied to ensure well-being is like asking how much well-being constitutes well-being? To define well-being is to list the criteria in the light of which comparative estimates may be made. To ask for more is to misunderstand the meaning of the term and the functions that it can legitimately serve in human discourse.

If I am correct, the basic and universal human needs or desires whose fulfillment constitutes well-being can be classified under four heads.

1. The first of these is health (and absence of physical disability or pain) with all that is required to maintain it—adequate food, shelter, medical care, etc. Health is so indisputably universal an object of human striving and its benefits are so obvious that I shall list it here without much further comment. I do wish, however, to observe that in listing health as a universal human need and urging its adoption as a criterion for estimating individual well-being, it is not implied that a man cannot enjoy a substantial measure of well-being even though his health is imperfect. Nor is it implied that ill-health cannot be a necessary or highly favorable condition for the enjoyment of certain other human goods. Although most of us would tend to regard as somewhat morbid the satisfactions Marcel Proust describes and

attributes to his ill-health in *Remembrance of Things Past,* it is quite possible that some physical ills do make available satisfactions of a kind unavailable to a man in good health. What I wish to say is simply (a) that good health is a necessary condition of satisfactions whose loss cannot be experienced without serious regret by any but a negligible fraction of mankind and (b) that the satisfactions of which ill-health might be a necessary condition are of a kind that the vast majority of human beings are either incapable of experiencing or unable rationally to regard as adequate compensation for loss of health. Similar qualifications apply to the following three criteria.

2. The second basic need or desire of the individual is for warmth, good will, or respect in his dealings with fellow human beings. All men are members of some social organization and all have learned early in life the difficulty of achieving most of their goals in the face of indifference or hostility on the part of those with whom they are obliged to deal. And only a few have failed to learn how difficult it is to achieve the good will of others if they do not themselves reciprocate the feeling. Apart from the value of mutual good will as a means to the achievement of other goals, however, it is almost universally appreciated as a good in itself. No one who has known it fully reconciles himself to its loss, and there is considerable evidence that even those who have not known it long for it intensely. The urgency of the need may be mitigated; but even the Stoics and Epicureans, who went further than any other major philosophical schools of the Western tradition in preaching detachment from finite and mortal objects, implicitly recognized its importance by ranking friendship among the highest of human values.

3. The third criterion is a reasonable balance between the individual's aspirations and the objective possibility of moving toward his goals. For the sake of brevity, though this involves some departure from ordinary usage, I shall use the term "contentment" to refer to the appropriate balance. This criterion, with its reference to "reasonable" or "appropriate" balance, is deliberately vague. Some ambitious, adventure-seeking individuals can support without discomfort and often even demand far

greater challenges than others. But everyone has a maximum frustration level; we can stretch only so far toward the achievement of envisaged goals without experiencing pain or acute discomfort. At the other end of the scale are some unenterprising, almost bovine types who demand little of life and accommodate themselves easily to an existence without serious challenge or adventure. But, again, men are not cows, and there is a point beyond which aimlessness or leisureliness becomes insupportable boredom. Man, as Aristotle and in modern times Dewey have rightly pointed out, is by nature an active being: a flabby psyche is no less disagreeable than a flabby body. Where on the scale between insupportable boredom and intolerable frustration contentment ought to be located will depend on the individual. But clearly everyone wants to be contented. Everyone desires not to suffer from an improper balance between what he is and what he would like to be, between what he has and what he wants, whether this imbalance takes the form of frustration and undue strain or boredom and absence of purpose.

The foregoing characterization of contentment is largely negative. Contentment is not, however, without its positive aspect. This may be described as the sense of power and self-expansion that comes from relatively unimpeded progress toward the goals we have set for ourselves. This sense of power and self-expansion does not depend to any great extent upon the concrete content of the goals chosen. The concrete objects of possible human striving may fall short of infinity, but they are at the very least astronomical in number. It must, however, be observed that striving toward chosen goals produces a positive state of contentment only if it calls into play a considerable number of the individual's native powers or capacities. A man who is highly endowed intellectually would not be content if his goals were of a kind which even a moron could achieve, nor would a man with the keen sensitivities of an artist be content with a life work devoted to the manufacture of glue. A person may resign himself to such activities, but resignation is not contentment, since the former involves a strong sense of regret whereas the latter does not.

4. Finally, as the fourth criterion, I list pleasures. By "a pleas-

ure" here I mean any relatively short-lived satisfaction of which we are immediately conscious throughout its duration. I mean to include not only the so-called lower pleasures, such as sexual gratification and the delectations of the palate, but also the so-called higher pleasures, such as aesthetic delight, the joys of creation, and great moments of romantic love or exalted friendship. The satisfactions of health, good will, and contentment do not qualify as pleasures in my sense of that term. These satisfactions are more prolonged than pleasures, and they do not make as insistent a claim upon our consciousness while we are experiencing them. In fact, their value is often most apparent to us when we have lost them.

What concrete kinds of pleasures contribute to personal well-being and how many of them must be experienced to assure well-being are again questions for which there are no precise answers. As to the kinds of pleasures, I say simply that any pleasure the individual is capable of experiencing qualifies, provided that it be rational for him to pursue it, *i.e.*, that he is not obliged to pay too high a price for it. As to the number of pleasures required I say only that in general this will be a function of the knowledge one possesses about one's capacities for experiencing pleasures, plus the intensity of the pleasures readily available. Other things being equal, the more aware one is of being able to experience a given pleasure, the more difficult it is to renounce it without distress. The immediate availability of other pleasures, however, especially if they are intense, will normally blunt our awareness of pleasures beyond reach and more or less fully compensate for their loss.

The point I wish to emphasize is that a life characterized by health and absence of physical pain, by good will in dealings with others, and by an active pursuit of goals toward which one can progress without undue stress falls short of genuine well-being. Pleasures are what give life relish, and though most men would, if necessary, sacrifice pleasure for the sake of health, good will, or contentment, few if any would ever fully reconcile themselves to its loss. In this respect the sacrifice of pleasure itself is markedly different from the sacrifice of one pleasure for another.

It might be questioned whether this classification of the elements in well-being is exhaustive, particularly in view of my avowed intention to include all those satisfactions that the vast majority of human beings could not forego without a sense of lasting regret. Some of the other possible candidates for inclusion are freedom, dignity, self-esteem, and a sense of personal identity. As I shall attempt to show in Chapter VII, however, these values are by-products of those already named. Still other candidates are a sense of cosmic purpose favorable to the achievement of human goals and an assurance of personal immortality. A consideration of these alleged values will have to await the discussion of religion in Chapter VIII.

RATIONALITY AND PERSONAL WELL-BEING

The obstacles that stand in the way of personal well-being under existing circumstances are for all but a favored few almost too numerous to catalogue, and a large number of these are obviously beyond individual rational control. For instance, half the world's population lacks the basic needs of health and without concerted social effort has little or no opportunity of securing them; whereas the other half enjoys these benefits largely at the cost of harshly competitive economic systems or repressive political controls that breed distrust and suspicion, of a division of labor that condemns large numbers of persons to uncreative and often demeaning work activities, and of a transformation in the physical environment that offends the most elementary aesthetic sensibilities. The peculiar conception of human well-being and of reason that led many classical thinkers, most notably the Stoics and Epicureans, to insist that the rational man could always triumph over difficulties of this order has seen its day. The inner resources of the individual human being, no matter how rational or disciplined, have their limits, and it is no part of my intention to flout common sense by denying them. On the contrary, a very important theme in this book is the necessity for more responsible and effective efforts at social reform, a theme that rests squarely upon a recognition of the general inadequacy of isolated individual effort.

If, however, the classical world generally erred through overestimating the benefits of personal rational discipline, the contemporary world tends to err by underestimation. And paradoxically the mistaken beliefs responsible for the excessive minimization of the powers of individual rational effort can be traced to classical sources. In their desire to establish their own conceptions of well-being and rationality, traditional philosophers seriously undermined the largely commonsensical conceptions of well-being and rationality I have presented here; and although contemporary thinkers have rejected the traditionalists' positive teachings—rationality as contemplation of eternal essences and well-being as detachment from worldly concerns—they have tended to accept uncritically their negative conclusions.

One of the more serious of these idols of the theater might be called the itch-scratch view of pleasure. In this view few, if any, pleasures could be an object of rational striving, since pleasures are impure in the sense that corresponding pains are necessary conditions of their experience. To the pleasure of the palate corresponds the pain of hunger; to the pleasure of drink, thirst; to the pleasure of sexual gratification, sexual frustration; etc. One cannot, therefore, hope to give one's life a dominantly pleasurable tone through rational effort; reason's job is to expose the vanity of this hope. When Freud defined pleasure as a modification of the level of tension, he was simply carrying on this tradition, and much of his pessimism has its source there.

The weakness of this view is obvious upon a moment's serious consideration. Most pleasures simply do not have corresponding pains. What pain, for instance, corresponds to the pleasure of listening to a Beethoven quartet expertly played? And even where the so-called physical pleasures are involved—and it is here that the argument has the greatest initial plausibility—the view does not hold up. Where hunger is sufficiently intense to be painful, there is little or no pleasure in eating; there is merely the frantic satisfaction of a pent-up need. And where there is pleasure in eating, the hunger that precedes is so far from being painful that it would be an exaggeration to speak even of slight discomfort. A normally constituted and moderately imaginative human being is, in fact, often able to derive pleasure from the deliberate postponement of physical gratification.

Another view that unduly minimizes the possibility of achieving well-being through personal effort might be called the treadmill theory of human striving. According to this theory there is no natural limit to the goals toward which men strive; as soon as one goal is achieved or some degree of a certain good obtained, another goal or a higher degree of that good tends to become an object of striving. The effect is a restless, unending pursuit from which no surcease is possible except in death. This view rightly recognizes that man is a naturally active being who can accept purposelessness for only brief stretches of time. But it wrongly presupposes that all striving is painful. For most persons purposeful striving is highly agreeable, especially if it involves a deployment of the higher faculties and if some measure of success can be reasonably anticipated. There is not only the sense of power and self-expansion of which I spoke earlier, but there is also the pleasure of anticipation where the goal itself is something pleasant and the satisfaction of knowing oneself respected for one's efforts where the goal is socially approved. Moreover, it is not altogether correct to say that there is no natural limit to the goals after which men strive. It is true, as noted above, that a wide variety of concrete goals may be and in fact are the object of human striving. It is also true that if the pursuit of chosen goals does not call into play the natural powers and abilities of the individual or if the achievement of the goals does not produce the satisfactions anticipated, the treadmill theory will fit the facts. Where, however, goals are wisely chosen, this is not the case; the rational man will tend to find a natural limit to his aspiration as he comes to form an accurate estimate of his own capacities and of objective possibilities.

A third view is that reason is merely instrumental in the sense that it can tell us how to achieve goals but cannot help us actually to choose them. Reason is concerned with means, not ends. Men pursue health, good will, contentment, and pleasure, not because of rational choice, but because they are so constituted that these goods produce satisfactions whose lack they cannot help experiencing with distress. These ends are given by nature rather than determined by the practice of rationality. Reason can and does confirm their existence as universal objects of striving, but its only practical role is to assist us in achieving them. Now, since these goals are often contradictory in that few individuals can simultaneously realize them all and since the resulting confusion of values is at least as great a source of human distress as frustration encountered in the pursuit of well-defined goals, the role of reason is sorely limited.

There is, of course, a grain of truth in this view. There can be no question that even the most rational of individuals are frequently prevented by external circumstance from simultaneously realizing all of their basic desires and that reason is often powerless fully to reconcile us to the loss of desired goods. But if we understand by "goals" or "ends" actual, concrete motives of personal behavior, then reason is no less relevant to the determination of ends than to the determination of means. Smith desires the good will of Jones. But is it rational for him to choose this goal? Is Jones the kind of person who will ever warm up to him? Smith desires to become a mathematics professor. But is this a rational goal? Has he the ability to succeed? Would he perhaps find greater use for his talents in another field? It is clear that these questions, which are all concerned with the choice of ends, are fully intelligible; that nothing but a knowledge of self, of others, and of environmental circumstance permit us to frame rational answers; and that our chances of attaining personal well-being depend as much upon our capacity to give rational answers to questions of this kind as upon our knowledge of means to the attainment of less problematic goals.

It is tempting to explain the tendency to see in reason nothing but a faculty for determining means to the achievement of goals as a result of failure to distinguish ultimate from subsidiary goals. Ultimate goals, it might be said, are given. Subsidiary goals are chosen. The person, however, who sees that ultimate goals are not objects of choice and who fails to distinguish between these and subsidiary goals might easily be led to deny that reason ever determines ends.

There is, however, a more accurate explanation for the unfortunate tendency to minimize the role of rational choice in shaping the ends we pursue. Any classification of ultimate goals or fundamental objects of human striving is highly formalized and abstract, so much so, in fact, that it is not a classification of goals or ends at all if by goals or ends one means concretely envisaged states of affairs operating as genuine motives of behavior. Human beings do not pursue good will in the abstract; they seek the good will of specific individuals or groups. Human beings do not desire contentment as such, but rather a specific set of activities that give proper scope to their abilities. Nor do they seek pleasure *tout court;* their goal is specific forms of pleasure. To the game of rational choice as played out concretely in real life a formal classification of ultimate human goals such as that proposed above is irrelevant. That classification was introduced for the sole purpose of helping us determine the role of reason in producing human well-being. It is, if you like, a statement of the formal conditions in the light of which we shall evaluate the success of the game of rational choice; these criteria are not themselves counters used in playing the game. In effect, we have said that we shall allow that the game of rational choice is worth playing only to the extent that the choices reason dictates lead to health, good will, contentment, and pleasure; but we have not committed ourselves to the view that men either do or should consciously and deliberately pursue goals so abstractly conceived. The simple fact is that men cannot do so. Unfortunately, the confusion between the criteria for evaluating an activity and the actual elements that are a part of that activity is all too common. In the present case the fallacy we wish to expose is the assumption that since for certain purposes reason may be formally considered merely a means to the achievement of well-being, reason is in fact concerned only with means. But to be a means to human well-being, reason need not concern itself exclusively with means. On the contrary, to be a means to human well-being, reason must be in a position to evaluate the relative merits of those concrete goals that are actually presented to it as possibilities. And when it is realized that a choice between even the most ultimate of *concrete* goals is not a choice between, say, pleasure per se and good will per se but between a specific kind of pleasure and the good will of a specific group, there is no more reason to deny the competence of reason to pass on ultimate goals than to pass on subsidiary goals.

There remains a fourth and final idol of the theater that has tended to reduce our confidence in reason as a means to personal well-being. Reason, it has often been said, is in no position to estimate the relative merits of desired but incompatible goals; for pleasures, satisfactions, values, or whatever you wish to call them are incommensurable. Rational preference for A over B implies the appraisal that A is a *greater* satisfaction than B, whereas rational refusal to pursue the positive value C implies the appraisal that its pursuit involves a negative, offsetting value D. But there is no rational method for weighing values or for determining when a given negative value offsets a given positive value. Rational preference and rational restraint are thus meaningless terms. Now, it must be granted that few if any practical tasks are more difficult than rationally to establish and defend a personal scale of values. It must also be granted that there is no fully satisfactory theoretical explanation of the process by which values are compared or hierarchically organized. But practical difficulties are not theoretical impossibilities, and the lack of a satisfactory theoretical explanation of the process by which values are compared does not constitute evidence for the nonrationality of the process.

All of us do constantly make statements such as, "Bach gives me greater pleasure than Brahms," or "The satisfaction of hearing *Aida* is not worth the discomfort of queuing up for several hours." And all of us agree that statements of this kind may be either true or false. We can all easily picture circumstances under which we would feel warranted in accepting such statements as true or, on the other hand, in believing that the speaker is mistaken or perhaps lying. If, however, satisfactions were incommensurable, if there were no rational method for comparing positive values or offsetting negative values against positive values, then we could not meaningfully qualify these statements as true or false; for it is universally agreed that where a statement can be correctly qualified as true or false there exists a rational method for determining the existence or nonexistence of what the statement purports to denote.

It seems, then, that those who claim that rational comparison of values is impossible even in principle cannot be taken seriously. When such claims are made in ordinary discourse they are hardly more than exclamations of impatience due to practical difficulties in determining the relative standing of specific values. When encountered in philosophical literature they are usually due to an unjustifiably narrow interpretation of rational procedures. Rational procedures are equated with scientific procedures and scientific procedures, in turn, with procedures employed in the highly developed physical sciences. One philosopher, for instance, argued against the utilitarian doctrine according to which we ought to produce a maximum of pleasure for the greatest number of persons by telling us that "it is impossible to measure amounts of pleasure in the way that we can measure amounts of heat or energy."[1] For persons who make a fetish of mathematical exactitude, an argument of this kind carries great weight. None the less, the argument rests upon a very elementary fallacy. If pleasures are as different from physical objects as the argument rightly presupposes, then the impossibility of measuring pleasures in the way that we measure physical entities is not at all surprising. Why should very different kinds of things be measured in the same way? Of course, if one makes the additional assumption that there is only one kind of measurement, the argument would be valid. But this assumption is wholly gratuitous. None of us does in actual practice hesitate to weigh the relative merits of different envisaged goals or to consider the success with which this is done an important part of wisdom. Moreover, those who have critically

[1] P. H. Nowell-Smith, *Ethics* (London: Penguin Books Ltd., 1954), p. 17.

examined the concept of measurement as employed in the natural sciences have discovered, often to their surprise, that even in this restricted area the concept has more than one meaning.

RATIONALITY AND SOCIAL WELL-BEING

In the largest sense of the term the good society is one which assures the maximum possible personal well-being for the maximum number of individuals. And if my task were either to appraise or to improve any given society, I would have to determine the desirability and/or necessity of all those institutions that in any way contribute to or impede its members' physical well-being, mutual good will, contentment, and pleasure. My task here, however, is the more modest one of determining whether the general practice of rationality contributes to the public welfare. In particular, I shall be concerned with deciding whether it is in the interest of society to encourage public debate on controversial issues in the schools, by means of the mass media of communication, or by any other methods. Although there are other ways in which society may encourage the practice of rationality, the most frequently employed as well as the most effective social means for encouraging or restricting the formation of rational judgment has always been the granting or withholding of freedom of expression. Moreover, arguments used to support other social methods for discouraging the practice of rationality—*e.g.*, opposition to universal and compulsory education—are almost invariably similar to those used in favor of restricting freedom of expression, so that little is lost by giving the discussion this more limited focus.

One of the most common arguments in favor of discouraging public debate turns on the assumption that social stability depends upon universal respect for tradition and constituted authority. This respect, it is said, will be lost if points of view contrary to tradition and constituted authority are allowed a full hearing.

This argument is vulnerable on several points. First, social stability could depend upon respect for tradition and constituted authority only to the extent that the traditions and the ruling elite of the society in question are capable of ensuring survival in the face of changing historical conditions. But since traditions and tradition-bound elites rarely evolve as rapidly as impersonal historical forces—*e.g.*, technological advance—a society is most unlikely to survive if it does not institutionally allow criticism of tradition and ruling cliques.

Second, stability by itself is not a valid social goal. The valid social goal is orderly progress, which is virtually impossible without freedom of expression. Every society harbors grave and long-standing social injustices. Almost invariably these injustices have been perpetuated because powerful groups have found that they serve their selfish ends, and almost invariably these powerful interest groups have rationalized their selfishness and foisted some false ideological tenet upon the general public. Without public debate and criticism of traditional points of view one cannot, therefore, reasonably expect orderly progress in so far as this involves the correction of social injustice.

Finally, the idea that social instability is a product of popular disrespect for one harmonious set of traditions or a single ruling elite is almost wholly false. More often than not social instability is a product of the fact that every society has several distinct and conflicting traditions or several distinct and competing power groups who together constitute its ruling elite. When the several powerful interest groups can no longer compromise their differences, the instability assumes crisis proportions. And as even the most cursory study of history reveals, a heavy contributor to every internal crisis is blind and fanatical loyalty to what is described as the country's best traditions. The point is not that a country is without good and bad traditions, but rather that only rational methods permit us to sort out the good from the bad. How, for instance, was the German officer corps to have decided whether the tradition of obedience to one's superiors or the tradition of respect for the rights of conquered peoples should prevail? How is the Southerner in the United States today to choose between the tradition of white supremacy and the tradition of respect for law?

Another related argument is that, given the complexity of social issues, the inevitable narrowness of individual experience, and the feebleness of the human intellect, unlimited public debate merely replaces comfortable certainties and decisiveness in behavior with gnawing doubts and indecisiveness. The appeal to respected authority is not only socially indispensable in the interest of stability but also essential to the individual's peace of mind. Now, it is unquestionably true that the person who has heard all sides of an issue is more likely to suspend judgment than the person who has not, that a state of suspended judgment or doubt on matters of any importance is in itself less agreeable than a state of firm conviction, and that individuals are often in no position to make important decisions without an appeal to expert authority. There are, however, three objections to this argument.

1. How is a person to recognize the limitations of his private experience and of his own intelligence except by the practice of rationality? Is it the rational man or the irrational man who believes himself competent to treat his physical maladies with homemade remedies? Is it the person who has heard the case for and against many points of view or the person who has heard only one side of each case who is likely to repose excessive confidence in his own powers of reasoning? Since the opinions of respected authority are easily assimilated, especially in early life, the individual who is not challenged to defend his views or who is not aware that other views exist will almost inevitably come to repose excessive confidence in his own opinions simply because they are his. The bigot, although his views derive from external authority, does not necessarily appeal to external authority. As often as not, no other authority is involved than his own private feeling of certainty.

2. If it is granted that the appeal to authority is usually made with respect to issues that the individual recognizes to be beyond his competence to decide, are we justified in assuming that it will produce mental comfort? In some cases, such as medicine, where the criteria of expertise are relatively clear, the individual may

be reasonably confident that he has chosen his authority wisely. Where, however, there are no sharply defined criteria in the light of which one may determine who is a competent authority, as is ordinarily the case in those areas where restriction upon freedom of speech is proposed, the appeal to authority involves a deliberate, perpetually renewed act of faith that borders on fanaticism and that merely transmutes, without abolishing, the discomfort of doubt.

3. The issues that arouse public debate are almost invariably of great practical consequence, issues about which it is humanly important to know the truth. If, therefore, there is even a modest chance that discussion and debate will lead to more adequate understanding, any attendant discomfort of doubt is surely worth enduring.

RATIONALITY AND SOCIAL REFORM

Many persons, especially in the Anglo-American liberal tradition, will readily grant that orderly social progress depends upon the existence of conditions favoring genuine public debate of controversial issues. And, supposing the existence of such conditions, these liberals would probably find no insuperable barrier to the acceptance of a moral criterion that limits the individual's responsibility to the rational pursuit of self-interest. Where, however, social conditions discourage public debate to the extent that few individuals could conceivably find it in their interest to raise their voices on behalf of social improvement, it might well be felt that the moral criterion of rational self-interest blocks progress. Under the latter conditions, widespread acceptance of my moral criterion means that progress, if it occurred at all, would be a result of historical accidents or of violent revolutionary activity. The only hope of peaceful and orderly progress under these conditions would be the willingness of individual men and women publicly to protest social injustice and to recommend needed reforms regardless of cost to themselves, which is precisely what a moral criterion of rational self-interest discourages.

It should at once be pointed out that this argument as stated is self-contradictory, for if the initial premise to the effect that social conditions favoring public debate constitute a *necessary condition* of orderly social progress is true, then the optimistic hope that orderly social progress can be achieved through the heroic, unrewarded efforts of social reformers whose activities are limited to public protest of social injustice and verbal recommendations with respect to needed reforms must be false. As, indeed, it is. The first step taken by totalitarian regimes is to render ineffective any merely verbal protests against its policies. The would-be social reformer does not take long to discover that he has no audience either because he is in jail or because his potential audience shuns him out of fear. If the regime is to topple, it will have to be through historical accidents, such as defeat in war (as in the case of Hitler's regime) or revolutionary activity (as in the case of Batista's). It should also be pointed out that as hope in the possibility of peaceful and orderly progress under adverse circumstances waxes, the sense of urgency with respect to the necessity of abolishing these adverse circumstances wanes. This form of optimism means political ineffectiveness. Widespread respect, or at the very least tolerance, of the social critic is a necessary condition of orderly social progress, and realistic appreciation of this elementary fact is an equally necessary condition of the same end.

The terms in which this problem has been posed are, however, not altogether satisfactory. My purpose is not to determine if or under what circumstances violence as opposed to the more peaceful method of free public discussion can or should be used to promote social betterment, nor is it to expose the emptiness of the current liberal rhetoric with its indiscriminate and often sanctimonious condemnation of violence. My purpose is to decide whether the advocacy of rational self-interest as a moral criterion will tend to inspire or to discourage efforts toward social reform in those societies where advocacy of this criterion is itself feasible.

Now, such societies are not adequately described simply as societies favoring public discussion; for although these societies differ from totalitarian societies in that enough freedom is granted the individual that he may reasonably hope to contribute to social betterment through nonviolent methods and without ultimate sacrifice of self-interest, it is none the less the case that even the freest of these societies imposes heavy penalties upon the social reformer. Powerful selfish interests and popular prejudice cannot be fought with impunity. The question thus is whether a more widespread adoption of my moral outlook would or would not tend to produce personalities who found it in their best over-all interests to work for social reform and who are prepared to endure the partial or short-term sacrifices that their best over-all interests demand.

Those who fear the adoption of my criterion are likely to argue that without sympathy or compassion for our fellow men we are not likely to make the requisite sacrifices and that a moral criterion that bids us refrain from acting upon these impulses when by doing so we defeat our own best interests will soon lead to their atrophy. The generous, benevolent, other-regarding dispositions must be reinforced and stimulated by the use of moral sanctions. Compassion and love are not, however, easily commanded or checked by moral sanctions. It is an understatement to say that neither the parent who demands love from his children as an obligation nor the totalitarians who attempt to motivate personal sacrifices by preaching the superior worth of the community have been notably successful. The generous, other-regarding dispositions are largely products of social institutions that engender mutual respect and that permit the individual rationally to regard himself as a full-fledged member of the community.

The initial plausibility of this objection is further reduced when we recognize that compassion for the victims of injustice neither is in fact nor can be in principle the most important factor motivating successful social reformers. It is no accident that conservatives tend to deprecate reason—consider Edmund Burke and his contemporary counterpart Russell Kirk, both of whose works are peppered with references to "puny reason"—whereas liberals are saddled with the appelation of "intellectuals." This is not only because effective social reform requires a high degree of rational labor but also and chiefly because the major prop of social injustice is an ideological façade or moral rhetoric in which the individual has been indoctrinated at a tender age and from which only rational discipline can emancipate him. Compassion for others when not combined with mental acuity reduces to useless sentimentality. Only rational men with their disgust for bias in the presentation of data bearing on social issues, for inconsistencies in the ideological justifications of current practice, for propagandistic appeals to the basest of human emotions, for obscurantism, for dogmatism, and for hypocrisy can be expected to make substantial contributions to the cause of human betterment.

chapter six

RATIONALITY AND MORAL CHARACTER

The position presented in this study clashes sharply with ingrained habits of thinking in which the moral and the rational are sharply separated—habits of thinking that reach back beyond Pauline Christianity to the Biblical myth according to which man was beguiled from a state of innocence by eating from the tree of knowledge. The seat of righteousness, it is said, lies in the heart rather than in the head. The key to moral maturity is a "good will," not rationality. Carried to its extremes, these distinctions, as one contemporary philosopher writes, lead to

> a division of men into two classes: in one class the wolves and the serpents, in the other the sheep and the doves; in one class the "clever rogue," or the "astute diplomat," shrewd but unscrupulous, in the other, "the simple honest man," or "simple rustic," naively scrupulous. The popular mind finds it difficut to believe that a "brainy" man can be altogether honest or that an honest man can fail to be somewhat deficient in "brains."[1]

The major purpose of this chapter is to expose the baselessness of these habits of thinking. I will not argue that a man of superior moral stature lacks feeling or that a man with superior rational powers could not use those powers to achieve morally undesirable goals. I will, however, argue that thought and feeling are not easily compartmentalized and that distrust of reason cannot but have adverse effects on moral character.

[1] Warner Fite, *The Examined Life* (Bloomington: Indiana University Press, 1957), pp. 107–08.

SOME MISTAKEN NOTIONS

The position I am arguing against has a variety of sources, one of them the traditional association of reason with pure reflectiveness or mere logicality. Reason's function on this traditional interpretation is disinterested contemplation, not the resolution of urgent personal and social problems. My own views on this subject have already been presented, and to the extent that they are acceptable, the popular dichotomy between the moral and the rational will be shaken; rationality on my interpretation being nothing other than a set of habitual dispositions whose worth consists precisely in their aptitude to promote human well-being.

The traditional view of reason, though it helps to explain the tendency sharply to separate the moral and the rational, fails to explain why rationality should be regarded with such deep suspicion, for when reason is conceived as a purely contemplative faculty it is not so much hostile as indifferent to morals. The moral taint that so often attaches to reason must be otherwise explained. A part of that explanation is that when rationality is interpreted as a means of promoting human well-being, it is the well-being of the individual agent, not of humankind as such, that is seen as primarily in question. A man who is believed to further his own well-being at the expense of others would in all likelihood be qualified as immoral, but not as irrational. My views on this subject have also been presented, and to the extent that they are acceptable, reason will be vindicated. For if I am right, the rational pursuit of one's own best long-range interests can rarely if ever be rightly regarded as detrimental to the best long-range interests of society as a whole; and if or when it could, the appropriate moral reaction is not to berate the man who exercises his right to the pursuit of happiness but rather to dedicate ourselves to the creation of a social order in which the interests of all individuals may be more fully harmonized.

There is, however, still another source, closely allied to the foregoing, for the popular suspicion of rationality. Some aspects of the problems that emerge here have been dealt with in previous chapters, but these problems are sufficiently important to warrant more detailed examination. What I have in mind is the view that in the development of desirable character traits, such as honesty, modesty, courage, tolerance, and compassion, rationality plays only a subsidiary role or that once such traits have been developed the practice of rationality tends to weaken them. Though this view has often been heatedly proclaimed, it has rarely been stated or defended with precision. It would appear, however, that the view derives its support from several different types of considerations.

1. With few exceptions, morally desirable character traits, or, to use an old-fashioned word, virtues, involve some degree of sacrifice. If one is honest, one must forego opportunities for personal gain; if one is courageous, one must risk one's life or reputation; if one is generous, one must part with something one considers valuable; etc. Now, if one believes that ultimate sacrifices are sometimes required in the name of morality, the rational man as we have defined him will probably not possess these virtues in the requisite degree; for the rational man does not cultivate and nourish character traits that he esteems to be contrary to his best over-all interests. With this set of ideas I shall not be concerned here; the argument of Chapter I should take care of them.

2. To effect a satisfactory reconciliation of the interests of individuals within any given society it is necessary to maintain a system of rewards and punishments, *i.e.*, to make it a matter of self-interest to each individual that he observe certain general rules of behavior. Positive sanctions or rewards for observance of these rules are ideally preferable to negative sanctions or penalties, but for obvious practical reasons the latter will continue to play a large role in the foreseeable future. These sanctions may take many forms and may be classified in many ways; as examples we may take simply economic, penal, and moral sanctions (praise

or blame). Now, it is conceivable that the practice of rationality would render a man exempt from this system of rewards and punishments, since by the practice of rationality a man might become adept at giving the impression of observing established rules, thereby escaping sanctions for their nonobservance, while at the same time violating the rules and profiting from their violation.

The weakness of this argument consists not in what is said, but in what is overlooked. For although it is true that the rational man is, other things being equal, better able to violate moral rules without detection, the nonrational man is at least as subject to the suspicion of violating the moral code precisely because he is not sufficiently rational to foresee that he will be detected or to act upon what knowledge he does possess. Generalizations of this kind are, of course, hazardous, but is it not reasonable to believe that every rationally planned crime whose author remained undetected is matched by at least one crime that would never have been committed were it not for the agent's failure rationally to consider the consequences of the act. In the case of killings, for which empirical data is available, there can be no question that rashly conceived or even blindly impulsive acts far outnumber those due to rational deliberation. Similarly, it is reasonable to believe that for every man who chose a life of crime because this kind of life promised the greatest chance of personal well-being, there is at least one other who chose it because he was insufficiently rational to foresee its disadvantages or to resist the lure of immediate temptation. The overwhelming consensus of opinion among those who deal professionally with criminals strongly supports this contention. Though, therefore, it must be conceded that the rational man has greater chances of escaping detection for wrongdoing, this does not mean that the rational man is legitimately *more* suspect of wrongdoing than the nonrational man. It means only that a policy of promoting rationality involves risks—risks, however, which are well worth taking in view of the more serious risks inherent in alternative policies.

3. A third argument is similar to the last in that it presupposes the importance of external sanctions in securing observance of

moral rules and sees in rationality a means by which the individual frees himself from their restraining influence. Here, however, the argument is not that the individual exempts himself from these sanctions by devising means of escaping detection for wrongdoing. The argument is rather that the individual becomes indifferent to the rewards and punishments that society finds it convenient to impose, acquiring such independence of mind and self-sufficiency that the opinion of others means little to him, that even poverty and imprisonment cease to arouse his fears.

This view has greater initial plausibility when rationality is conceived in traditional terms. Even when rationality is conceived as I conceive it, however, the argument is not without plausibility, especially in so far as moral sanctions are concerned, for undeniably the practice of rationality will tend to produce indifference and perhaps even contempt with regard to what Socrates called "the opinion of the many." One need not make any great progress as a rational being before discovering that the moral beliefs and attitudes of "the many" are often no more than inherited prejudices; and having made this discovery, one is not likely to respond to their expressions of praise or blame as frequently or as promptly as one had previously. To the extent therefore that society attempts to control our behavior by appealing to our desire for general social respect (or fear of social disapprobation) and to the extent that observance of the conventional moral rules is socially desirable, rationality will be rightly seen as a threat to the moral life.

But how serious is that danger? And does the adoption of my moral criterion not have advantages that neutralize it? If the prevailing moral rules are rationally well founded, is it not likely that this will be discovered by the practice of rationality, and is it not better that the individual adheres to them because he knows the arguments that make it reasonable to do so rather than because of pure prejudice or fear of disapproval? If, on the other hand, the conventional moral rules are not acceptable to the rational conscience of the individual, is it not better that he protests against their imposition than that he accept them slavishly out of fear?

Moral sanctions do, in fact, rank among the weapons used to produce adherence to moral rules, and often rightfully so. With adults who are either unable or unwilling to use their rational faculties no less than with children below the age of reason, sanctions are sometimes very helpful. But to blame an adult human being with normal rational faculties for behavior that he believes to be dictated by reason constitutes an affront to human dignity and a social danger of the first magnitude. If indifference to, or even contempt for, the opinions that prevail in one's society is a sign of shamelessness or moral weakness, then the antifascist in Nazi Germany and the white integrationist in the South of the United States today will have to bear the label. Moral progress depends upon the ability and the willingness of individual human beings to subject conventional views to critical examination, and moral progress will be painfully slow until a sizable number of individuals liberate themselves from undue fear of social disapproval and until society learns that the individual's integrity as a rational being is a greater value than sensitivity to the approval or disapproval of others.

Edmund Burke, the father of almost all modern conservative thought, was not altogether incorrect when he said that the "moral sentiments, so nearly connected with early prejudice as to be almost one and the same thing, will assuredly not live long under a discipline which has for its basis the destruction of all prejudices."[2] But in an age when we have learned to what horrors early prejudices can lead, we should not be greatly disturbed by a discipline whose object is to distinguish between them and the "moral sentiments" to which they would otherwise be assimilated and that give them the cover of respectability.

4. Although respect for conventional moral rules and the development of personality traits corresponding to these rules is to some extent fostered and maintained by a system of rewards and penalties that appeal to the individual's self-interests, it is often said that other and more important factors are involved. A man

2 Edmund Burke, *An Appeal from the New to the Old Whigs*, 3rd ed., (London: 1891), p. 136 (first pub. 1790).

does not tell the truth simply because it is ultimately in his interests to do so. It has, in fact, often been maintained that the man who tells the truth for reasons of self-interest is not acting morally at all. His behavior is too hollow, too cold, too rational. Morality must be rooted in the feelings; only deep-seated emotional factors can account for the strength of mankind's attachment to moral ideals.

Unfortunately, persons who argue in this way are most often extremely reluctant to specify the emotional factors involved or to explain why the practice of rationality should in any way threaten their vitality. All too often, they feel they have done their whole duty by dubbing these feelings with the name "moral"; and all too often antagonism between reason and passion is gratuitously assumed. Moreover, it should be borne in mind that whatever validity this line of criticism might have when directed against some positions that stress the role of rationality and self-interest in promoting right conduct, it has considerably less when directed against the position taken in this book. As will be recalled from Chapter II, I freely grant that nonrational factors, such as the warm-hearted regard of our fellow men induced by social circumstance, play a great role in the genesis of moral dispositions; that moral dispositions, being to some extent habitual, often carry with them an element of spontaneity or nonreflectiveness; and finally that the knowledge in the light of which commendable moral dispositions are formed includes not only abstract (cold) knowledge but also concrete (warm) knowledge, which is as much a product of our imaginative as of our purely ratiocinative powers. I have also insisted on several occasions that the function of reason is not, as many traditional philosophers maintained, to banish passion or to extricate us from its coils, but rather to direct or control, to refine or to purify, the passions. Even so, there are forms that this general line of criticism takes which are worthy of further examination.

According to one view, the causes of any given moral disposition are almost infinitely complex. If we are honest, it is not because we believe that it is in our self-interest crudely conceived to be honest or even because we have come to value harmonious relationships with our fellow man and feel more or less intuitively that these relationships will be jeopardized by an act of deception on our part. It is because honesty is an element in Christian ethics or in the American tradition with which we identify ourselves; because persons whom we admire are honest or have exhorted us to be honest, and we wish to model our lives after them or their dictates; because, in brief, honesty has become a strand in the tightly woven fabric of our lives. This being the case, how can the practice of rationality fail to have a deleterious effect upon our moral dispositions? However reason is conceived, it is critical and analytic. It cannot fail to destroy the organic wholeness of the personality. Even if we resolutely exempted our moral beliefs and dispositions themselves from critical scrutiny, they would not be safe. The entire tone, the emotional tenor of our lives will be changed by habits of critical reflection; every time a cherished childhood belief goes by the board, there will be reverberations throughout the entire personality. We will become hollow, empty men.

Now, it must be granted that the human personality is a substantial unity, that a large number of causal factors of the type indicated do contribute to the formation of moral character, and that a modification of any element in the human personality could conceivably have a bearing upon other elements. It must also be granted that reason is a critical, analytic faculty which if fully exercised will almost invariably lead to the uprooting of cherished beliefs and habits. Finally, it must be granted that the uprooting of cherished beliefs rarely occurs without distress.

Several things, however, cannot be granted. First, unity itself, though no doubt a value, is not the overriding value presupposed by those who offer this kind of argument. The richness and moral quality of an individual's experience cannot be left out of consideration. If they were, an automaton thoroughly indocrinated in Nazi ideology would be the superior being he claimed to be. In the second place, though except in rare cases the individual human personality is highly integrated, its integration is never complete. To limit ourselves to only one aspect of the personality, our moral dispositions are no more integrated than the moral rules of which these dispositions are concrete incarnations are logically consistent. And how, if not by an appeal to reason, can we heal the rent in our personality that arises when our moral dispositions bid us act in two different ways with respect to the same situation?[3] If we cling resolutely to our moral dispositions in the face of numerous conflicts like these, we shall of course spare ourselves the pain of relinquishing our old personalities, but only by exposing ourselves to pains of another kind. Third, though it is true that reason is critical and analytic, reason is also constructive and synthetic. When, for instance, our moral rules or dispositions conflict, it is the function of reason not only to expose the contradiction but also to discover some means of mitigating the conflict either by an appeal to more fundamental principles that better reflect our total personality or by creating a mode of life from which situations that evoke these conflicts are absent. Ultimately, reason is more constructive than destructive; it destroys only to build anew.

[3] The following texts by Edmund Burke are eloquent testimony to the conservative's inability to deal with this problem:

> I admit, indeed, that in morals, as in all things else, difficulties will sometimes occur. Duties will sometimes cross one another. Then questions will arise: which of them is to be placed in subordination; which of them may be entirely superseded? These doubts give rise to that part of moral science called *casuistry*. . . . But the vary habit of stating these extreme cases is not very laudable or safe because, in general, it is not right to turn our duties into doubts. They are imposed to govern our conduct, not to exercise our ingenuity; and therefore, our opinions about them ought not to be in a state of fluctuation, but steady, sure and resolved. (*Ibid.*, pp. 101–02.)

> It is not worth our while to discuss, like sophisters, whether in no case some evil for the sake of some benefit is to be tolerated. Nothing universal can be rationally affirmed on any moral, or any political subject. Pure metaphysical abstraction does not belong to these matters. The lines of morality are not like the ideal lines of mathematics. They are broad and deep as well as long. They admit of exceptions; they demand modifications. These exceptions are not made by the process of logic, but by the rules of prudence. (*Ibid.*, p. 19.)

MORAL DISPOSITIONS AND INDIVIDUAL RATIONAL DISCIPLINE

More positively stated, my position is as follows: (1) The noncognitive factors essential to the development of a healthy moral character are in general worthless and often actually pernicious unless controlled and directed by individual rational discipline. (2) These noncognitive factors are not to any great extent a result of "moral education" in the narrow sense in which this term is most often employed; they are rather a product of larger social circumstance and can best be fostered through rational social policy. In this section I shall attempt to substantiate the first of these claims by considering specific moral dispositions or desirable character traits. My intention is not, of course, to give an exhaustive or detailed description of the many conventional virtues, but merely to expose the inadequacies inherent in the widespread tendency to regard them as primarily affective-conative dispositions having a largely subterranean existence on a nonrational level of the human personality. The pattern of my argument can be easily applied to virtues not explicitly discussed.

Consider, for example, the virtue of tolerance. In attempting to define "tolerance," as in attempting to define almost any term used to denote one of the accepted virtues, two problems are encountered. The first of these problems follows from the vagueness of the term. Few persons would hazard an explicit definition of it. There is, of course, a common core of meaning upon which general agreement could be secured. Everyone, for instance, would agree that the tolerant man shows a greater reluctance than the intolerant man either to pass judgment upon others or to impose negative sanctions upon persons whose conduct he believes wrong. None the less, any proposed definition of tolerance would, if thoroughly precise, be too broad or too narrow in the sense that it either included cases that many persons would want excluded or failed to include cases that many others would want included.

This incorrigible vagueness of the term is, however, a less serious problem than the second, *viz.*, that in employing the term we are often torn between a desire to remain true to ordinary usage despite its vagueness and a desire to use the term in an exclusively honorific sense. If, for instance, a man refused to pass judgment or to impose sanctions when we believed that he ought to do so, we are hard put to decide what to say. On the one hand, we are tempted to say: "But he is not tolerant at all; he is simply indulgent, morally flabby, irresponsible." On the other hand, we are tempted to say: "But he is overly tolerant," or "Tolerance is not as important a virtue as he thinks it is; there are others, such as righteous indignation, that ought to take precedence." Something may be lost, whichever course we adopt. If we refuse to grant that the man is acting tolerantly, we risk misunderstanding through a perhaps unwarranted departure from the conventional descriptive meaning of the term, whereas if we grant that the man is tolerant and *deplore* his tolerance we risk a failure of communication with those for whom the term is inviolably honorific. Fortunately persons who are fully aware of the double role of the term (*i.e.*, its simultaneously descriptive and honorific functions) will easily understand us whichever mode of speech we adopt, and, fortunately, my purposes do not require that I decide which mode of speech is generally preferable.

In fact, enough has already been said to permit me to make my point with respect to tolerance. If tolerance is defined descriptively as a relative reluctance to pass judgment upon others or to impose negative sanctions, then because of the obvious vagueness in the definition any alleged act of tolerance is seen to be genuinely virtuous only to the extent that a man *knows* when it is proper to pass judgment or to impose sanctions and can in the light of this knowledge rationally justify his act. The role of cognition in the moral life is vindicated, as is the uselessness of the noncognitive factor in tolerance without rational discipline. If, however, tolerance is used in a purely honorific sense, then we easily see that the very definition of tolerance must incorporate a reference to knowledge—tolerance becoming the tendency to withhold judgment or the imposition of sanctions when there is reason to believe that judgment would be rationally unwarranted or the imposition of sanctions useless for the purpose of achieving moral goals. Again the role of cognition is vindicated and the noncognitive factor in tolerance is recognized as valueless without rational discipline.

This point can be made in still another way. As Aristotle rightly pointed out, most virtues may be considered a mean between two extremes—a straight and narrow path from which it is all too easy to stray. Tolerance, for instance, may be considered a mean between overpermissiveness or moral insensibility on the one hand and excessive rigidity or punitiveness on the other. To keep to the narrow path of tolerance we must be alert to the dangers that await us both on the right and on the left. But how is this to be done? What could be more obvious than that pure feeling or rigid habit is incompetent to make the fine discriminations required? When we examine tolerance in this light it becomes evident that the injunction to be tolerant is well-nigh meaningless. We must be *intelligently* tolerant. The proper question is not "Ought we to be tolerant?" but rather "When, with whom, under what circumstances, and in what ways ought we to be tolerant?" The crudity of our ordinary ways of thinking about the conventional virtues and especially our lazy tendency to regard them as self-contained, psychic entities of a nonrational order stand mercilessly exposed. To be properly tolerant, one must know when in any concrete set of circumstances one has the right kind and the right amount of information to pass judgment on others, and not only when but what kinds of sanctions will be most effective—which offenses are best punished with imprisonment, which with dismissal from work or exclusion from professional activity, which with social ostracism or expressions of disapproval, etc.

The pattern of the analysis I have made of tolerance applies equally to almost all the other virtues, although I shall limit my discussion to three further examples—generosity, courage, and sincerity. Generosity is in a sense complementary to tolerance. The noncognitive element of the latter, *viz.*, the reluctance to pass judgment or to impose negative sanctions, expresses a more deep-seated disposition—an attitude of care with respect to others. The noncognitive element in generosity is a tendency to come to the aid of others and may be regarded as an expression of the same deep-seated disposition which underlies tolerance. Whereas, however, tolerance is the negative manifestation of that disposition, the unwillingness unnecessarily to inflict pain or discomfort; generosity is its positive manifestion, a disposition to give so that others may know comfort and pleasure. And it is as difficult to be intelligently generous as it is to be intelligently tolerant. At what point does the generous parent become overindulgent? How often do most of us, through failure of rational discipline, give too much, to the wrong persons or causes, at the wrong time, or in the wrong way? How often are we niggardly when careful consideration would reveal that our best long-range interests demand generosity?

And similarly with courage, which may be descriptively defined as the willingness to expose one's person or one's reputation to some kind of risk. The failure to be properly courageous, whether through excess fear or through rashness, is far more often due to imperfect understanding or failure of rational discipline than to sheer excess or deficiency of nerve. One need only consider the relatively small number of "cowards" encountered among army conscripts to realize how great is the average capacity for withstanding stress. And if that capacity reveals itself more conspicuously in times of national emergency when individuals are exposed to physical danger than in the ordinary peacetime conduct of life where the dangers are preponderantly moral, it is largely because the vast majority of human beings have not the mental culture to recognize the latter, less immediate and more insidious, though no less real, dangers to their personal development. The lack of moral courage that so often produces botched and maimed personalities is more often due to a lack of brains than a lack of guts. It is true, of course, that most men are obliged to wage their fight against personal degradation in the privacy and loneliness of their individual conscience, whereas the display of physical courage is usually rewarded with public plaudits. But this is only another way of saying that, whereas all of us have the wit to recognize physical cowardice or courage, few of us have the wit to recognize moral cowardice or courage. How many parents, spouses, friends, and children who appropriately support an individual when he is faced with psysical danger remain silent and without understanding when the same individual faces a moral crisis?

At first sight it might seem that any attempt to analyze sincerity or honesty (I shall not here be concerned with the nuances of meaning that sometimes lead us to differentiate between the two terms) in the foregoing manner would be highly artificial. It does, however, yield to this type of analysis as convincingly as tolerance, generosity, or courage. The descriptive core in this case is a tendency to represent truthfully one's beliefs and feelings. And if at first sight a definition in terms of this descriptive core seems wholly adequate, it is in great part because of the unfortunate popular prejudice that pictures beliefs and feelings as discrete, clearly defined items in human experience immediately available to introspective observation. But just how without rational discipline is John to know that he does in fact love Mary and that he is speaking the truth when he promises to cherish her until death does them part? How without the use of intelligence is one to know even what one means, much less whether one is speaking the truth, when one says that one believes in the existence of God. It is true that on occasion we express beliefs and feelings that can be discerned without fine intellectual discriminations or nicety of judgment, as when we report that we arrived late to work or were upset by a remark addressed to us. It is also true that cases of this kind are not without their importance. But it is perfectly clear that a man who is honest with respect to these cases alone would fall woefully short of the moral ideal. Furthermore, it should be observed that to be sincere not only must one know what one really believes and really feels, but also one must know when it is morally appropriate to express these beliefs and feelings. For with honesty, as with the other virtues discussed, one can err by excess as well as by deficiency. As examples we have not only the fanatic who will tell the truth even though it costs himself or another his life, but also the stranger on the train and the drunk in the bar who insist upon pouring out their life histories to us under circumstances such that the recital can do nobody any good.

One of the few exceptions to the foregoing pattern of analysis is the virtue of justice, impartiality, or fairness. (Again, I shall not take into account the subtle differences in meaning between these three terms, since these differences are irrelevant to the issues here under discussion.) Except under highly unusual circumstances we would not be tempted to speak of an excess of justice, nor do we often find ourselves in a situation where it would be necessary to choose between using the term in its ordinary descriptive meaning or using it in an unconventional but honorific manner. This does not mean, however, as I shall show presently, that justice is an easily practiced virtue requiring little in the way of knowledge or rational discipline. On the contrary, justice is exactly like the other virtues discussed in that it consists of an amalgam of cognitive and noncognitive elements.

Noncognitively justice consists in a disposition to take into account the interests of all persons or groups that are affected by one's behavior plus a disposition to suppress impulses to give preference to oneself for selfish reasons or to other persons simply because one has special sympathy for them. Attention must be called to the provisos in this definition. Justice obviously does not demand that an individual devote himself to the cultivation of all persons' well-being with the same seriousness that he does his own or that of his family and immediate associates. In fact, the contrary is the case. None the less, justice does clearly give precedence to the interests of the group as opposed to the individual and of larger groups as opposed to smaller groups. The explanation of this apparent dilemma lies in the fact that we usually assume the interests of larger groups to be best served when individuals pursue with special energy their personal interests or those of smaller groups. And in many cases this assumption is highly reasonable. It is, for instance, difficult to imagine an institution that better serves the interests of society as a whole than the family system with all that it involves in the way of preferential treatment of spouses toward one another and of parents toward children. What is unjust is preferential treatment for oneself or limited groups in cases where preferential treatment is believed to run counter to the well-being of society as a whole. A father may, for instance, at least in most societies, use his wealth to give his son exceptional educational advantages, but he ought not to use his influence to secure for his son exemption from military service. In the former case he would not be acting selfishly or giving preference to his son simply because of special sympathy for him; he is exercising prerogatives within the context of social institutions that are believed to be in the best interests of society as a whole. In the latter case, he would be acting selfishly and showing partiality because neither he nor society believes that the interests of the larger group can be served when individuals are allowed to show preference of this kind for friends or kin.

What then are the cognitive elements in the virtue of justice? At least four may be distinguished. Cognitively justice demands (1) knowledge of whose interests are affected by one's behavior, (2) knowledge of when preferential treatment for oneself or immediate associates conflicts with the interests of society as a whole, (3) knowledge of the psychological mechanisms that unduly tie us to self or friends, and (4) knowledge of means by which we can liberate ourselves from the confines of crude self-interest and parochial attachments. So far as the present argument goes, a man may want to be just without subjecting himself to rational discipline (though later I shall argue to the contrary), but it is already clear that the gap between wanting to be just and actually being just cannot be closed without an appeal to reason.

MORAL DISPOSITIONS AND SOCIAL CIRCUMSTANCES

In the last section I tried to show that the successful practice of the conventional virtues requires continuing rational discipline on the part of the individual, my intent being to correct the widespread tendency to stress brute habit and feeling at the expense of reason in the analysis of individual moral conduct. A necessary condition is not, however, to be confused with a sufficient condition, and though reason is necessary to the moral life it is obvious that nonrational, noncognitive elements are also required. In the present section I shall attempt to identify the primary noncognitive elements and to explain their origin. The crux of my position will be that the necessary noncognitive elements can be generally produced only through the adoption of wise social policies, as opposed to mere moral exhortation.

As the reader is already aware, one of the principal contentions in this study is that society does and ought to build moral character by an appeal to self-interest. In the words attributed to Pericles, "where the rewards for merit are greatest, there are found the best citizens."[4] I am not, of course, committed to the doctrine that men do invariably act so as to promote their personal self-interest; it is clear that men often do not do so, if for no other reasons than that frequently they do not know what constitutes true self-interest or else they succumb to the temptation of immediate satisfactions. Neither am I committed to the view that men are ineradicably selfish, i.e., that they are incapable of taking personal satisfaction in the well-being of others. None the less, it is clear that self-interest even narrowly conceived is a powerful motive that society must harness to serve its interests. Other things being equal, where crime does not pay there will be fewer criminals. Where honesty is rewarded and dishonesty punished, men will be more veracious. Despite the incontestable importance of self-love as a noncognitive factor leading to the practice of virtue, I shall not here emphasize it. My purpose here is rather to expose the inadequacy of the view that moral character is or ought ultimately to be built by an appeal to rational self-interest alone—a view that I may unwittingly have misled some readers into regarding as an adequate statement of my own position. This formula suggests that the moral task of society is

[4] *The Complete Writings of Thucydides,* trans. Crawley (New York: Random House, Inc.), p. 109.

merely to determine what are the interests of the individuals who constitute it, to ensure that they are aware of their true interests, and to devise a system of rewards and punishments that will eliminate or mitigate possible conflicts of interest. In fact, however, the moral task of society involves much more than this.

In the first place society must not only appeal to actually existing self-interests, it must also shape or create individual needs and desires. This is something that society inevitably does in any case merely by instituting a system of rewards and punishments; for if it is true that an effective system of rewards and punishments must be based upon a knowledge of what individuals do actually want or desire, it is no less true that to be effective this system must also actually influence the individual's concrete choice of goals. If, for instance, imprisonment for crime is to be an effective sanction, it must be the case that individuals do actually shun imprisonment, but it must also be the case that knowledge of possible imprisonment will cause individuals to regard contemplated crimes in a different light and to reshape accordingly their concrete desires. In this respect the view under criticism is misleading, but not actually false. In the second place—and it is here that the view in question completely breaks down—society neither does nor ought to shape individual needs and desires solely by the use of rewards and punishments. To harmonize individual interests other means are also required, and it is these other means with which I shall be principally concerned in this section.

First, however, a word must be said about the relative importance of moral as opposed to other sanctions in the development of moral character. Undoubtedly praise and blame are forms of reward and punishment which society may on occasion properly use. With the exception of totally psychopathic characters, men do generally desire the good will of their fellow men and will sometimes go to great lengths to avoid expressions of contempt or to gain the reward of a kindly word of approbation. At the same time men are often responsive to the emotively charged language in which expressions of approbation or disapprobation are usually couched, quite independently of any desire for prestige or fear of dislike. (Certainly some words have approbative or pejorative associations, and when these words are habitually used to refer to certain experiences our attitudes are affected. The man, for instance, who habitually hears the word "nigger" used will, other things being equal, tend to develop a negative attitude toward Negroes.) I am convinced, however, that both the effectiveness and the desirability of moral sanctions as a factor in moral education are grossly exaggerated.

First, responsiveness to the emotive aspects of language and the desire for social approbation usually occur relatively late in the individual's development, in many cases not until after some of the major directions of moral development have already been determined. A very young child who is told that an act is naughty will normally remain unmoved unless the speaker is in a position to punish him. Apparently for him the primary significance of the word is "act to be punished," not "act of which the speaker disapproves." When we speak of the relatively great sensitivity of children, we are not perhaps indulging in pure sentimentality, but it is undeniable that children are imperfectly socialized and imperfectly attentive to the nuances of language. And whatever adults may be tempted to say about children in the abstract, when it come to the concrete task of educating them, they rely far more heavily upon statements of fact—unfortunately, often false—than upon simple expressions of approval or disapproval: *e.g.*, "Crime never pays," "God will punish you for that," "Mother always knows when you are lying." Even in early adolescence in such emotionally charged areas as sex this is often true. Many parents deal with the masturbating child not so much with expressions of disgust or disapproval as with statements about the dire consequences to which the practice leads.

Second, among adults, whose sensitivity to emotively charged language and whose capacity for being pleased or pained by the attitudes of others are usually greater than among children, the effect of moral sanctions as a technique of moral education is seriously mitigated by two factors. (a) The typical adult seeks not indiscriminate approbation but rather the approbation of those he respects. And those he respects are more often than not those whose moral character approximates his own. The antitotalitarian will be either unmoved by the emotive language and violent expressions of contempt used by a Hitler or moved to develop his personality in the opposite direction. (b) For a person to be moved by the desire of approbation or by emotive language to adopt a certain mode of conduct, it is necessary that persons significant to him do in fact express approval of that mode of conduct and do in fact use emotive language intended to produce it. But it is precisely in those cases where most is expected of this technique that it is least likely to be used. Either a line of conduct serves the individual's best long-range interests or else it does not. If it does, the most effective technique of moral education is to point this out; the form of moral conditioning under discussion is merely a helpful auxiliary. If the conduct does not serve his best interests, most of us hesitate to berate him for not adopting it; not simply or even primarily because we believe that an expression of disapprobation would be relatively ineffective here (although this is a part of what is involved), but more importantly because most of us feel that a line of conduct worthy of social approbation ought to be rewarded by more than social approbation. If, for instance, an economic system is such that honesty puts an individual at a serious competitive disadvantage, the system is at least as much at fault as the dishonest individual, for honesty ought to pay not only with prestige but with profits. We hesitate to express disapproval of dishonesty in these circumstances because we do not know whether the dishonest individual is a relatively innocent victim of an evil society or a morally deficient member of a society to whose corruption he is contributing. A good case could be made either way, but the situation is not sufficiently clear-cut and the arguments for the former possibility are so strong that we hesitate to bring to bear the full weight of moral sanctions.

As to the desirability, or better, the undesirability, of extensive reliance upon moral sanctions my position was indicated in the first section of this chapter. The effectiveness of this method of moral education depends upon the individual's desire for social approbation and his responsiveness to the emotive aspects of language. But when these are carried beyond a certain point they become inimical to clear-headed and rational appraisal of social need and of true individual well-being, thereby undermining efforts directed toward the achievement of social reform and individual self-reliance. In the language of contemporary critics of American society, a society that relies heavily upon moral sanctions cannot but be dangerously conformist.

What, then, are the primary noncognitive factors in addition to self-love that account for the development of desirable moral character? In my opinion there are two others, benevolence and duty. The first of these, which appears to be involved in almost all of the moral dispositions but which is most conspicuously present in the so-called other-regarding virtues such as tolerance and generosity, was discussed in Chapter II. This is the tendency to be personally pleased or pained by the happiness or unhappiness of others. Its opposites are either indifference to others (want of warmth, sympathy, compassion) or else a tendency to experience positive satisfaction at the suffering of others (vindictiveness, malice, etc.). This tendency, which for want of a more convenient or accurate label I have called the spirit of benevolence, is obviously one that cannot be induced by an appeal to self-interest. A person may know that it is in his best interests to behave generously or tolerantly to others and consequently *act* generously or tolerantly, but no appeal to his best interests or knowledge of his best interests will make him *feel* benevolent. And as long as he does not *feel* benevolence, a valuable reinforcement to the appeal to self-interest will be lost, the personal feeling of pleasure or pain at the happiness or unhappiness of others being one of the factors to be taken into account in appraisals of self-interest. It is, therefore, extremely important that society do what it can to induce a spirit of benevolence among its members, to make its members experience the well-being of others as a goal to be cherished for its own sake and not merely as a means to personal well-being.

How is this to be done? The answer is that society must create a harmony of interests between its members such that the well-being more or less crudely conceived of one be favored by the well-being more or less crudely conceived of others. The little available empirical data lead me to believe that there is probably no inborn tendency for human beings to experience an affect of pleasure or pain at the happiness or unhappiness of others and that the growth of this tendency is closely correlated with a process of psychological association and what I earlier called hedonic spread by which the individual comes to link the well-being of others with the satisfaction of his own purely selfish desires. Children of parents who rarely experience moments of joy or whose moments of well-being are rarely occasions for treating their children to special attentions are far less likely to develop a spirit of benevolence than children of happier parents whose moments of optimum well-being are occasions for general family rejoicing. And a similar remark is in order with respect to children reared in institutions, where what little attention they receive is most often cold and impersonal. The reason for these facts is clear: these children have had little or no opportunity to associate their personal well-being with the well-being of others. For further confirmation of my contention consider the most commonly accepted explanation for the development of envy and vindictiveness, *viz.*, sibling rivalry resulting from a situation in which children are obliged to compete for favors and attention, the pleasures and satisfactions of one being purchased at the expense of the others.

As will be seen from the foregoing remarks, I have no quarrel with the current opinion of psychologists, who almost unanimously declare that an individual's capacity for experiencing benevolent sentiments is established at a tender age and depends to a great extent upon family circumstances. It would be a mistake, however, to conclude from this that society is powerless to foster benevolence or that social efforts to do so would necessarily involve impractical and objectionable forms of interference in private family life. On the one hand, although it is probably true that the capacity for benevolence cannot be fostered beyond a relatively early age, when the child's world is largely limited to the family, harshly competitive social institutions to which an individual is exposed later in life can do much to diminish that capacity after it has been established or to inhibit the individual from exercising it. It is even possible that the individual whose childhood experiences dispose him favorably toward benevolence will be so disillusioned upon entering the larger adult world that the effect of early training will be worse than undone and that, by what psychologists sometimes call a reaction formation, he will become notably vindictive. On the other hand, factors which indirectly dispose individuals toward benevolence, such as the happiness or well-being of their parents, are clearly factors that general social policy can favor. The selfishness of children is a general fact of nature, but when parents fail to provide favorable conditions for the moral development of their children it would be sheer fatuousness to hold nature responsible. Imperfect moral development of the individual must often be ascribed immediately to unfavorable childhood experiences, but ultimately it can be traced to general social conditions.

Although, as earlier pointed out, the spirit of benevolence most obviously underlies other-regarding virtues such as generosity and tolerance it is not without importance in other areas of moral experience. The benefits to other persons of virtues such as honesty or justice are so obvious that it would be very surprising if benevolence were not often among the motives leading to their adoption. None the less, it is clear that there can be no adequate understanding of such virtues as justice and honesty without analysis of what we call the sense of duty, the third primary noncognitive factor in moral character. It is true that the spirit of benevolence can be generalized beyond the limited social sphere to which it is most often confined; and it is tempting, for the sake of simplicity, to explain an individual's willingness in the name of duty to be honest or just, for example, even though he hurts himself, his family, or his immediate associates as a result of his having widened the sphere of his sympathies. This temptation must be resisted. Examples abound of cases in which the spirit of benevolence actually conflicts with the sense of duty: the judge who out of respect for law condemns a beloved son to death; the giver who is bidden by sympathy to distribute alms to beggars on the streets but who is bidden by duty to give to a large charitable organization that will make better use of the money; the statesman who feels obliged to sacrifice his own class interests for the sake of other classes, or his own generation for the sake of future generations; etc. Whatever the concrete analysis of the sense of duty may be and however true it may be that the sense of duty and the spirit of benevelence usually pull or push in the same direction, there can be no mistake that the sense of duty is a distinct motive existing independently of benevolence.

In the concrete analysis of the sense of duty only two things seem to be beyond dispute; first, the sense of duty involves respect for general rules; second, the violation of these rules causes the individual with a sense of duty to experience a loss of self-esteem while observance usually affords him a sense of self-respect.

The benevolent man is pleased by the happiness and pained by the distress of others. The righteous man by contrast is pleased or pained by his own observance or nonobservance of rules that he regards as authoritative, and his pleasure or pain is closely related to an image of himself as he would like to be. The great puzzle is to understand how and why men come to adopt an ideal self-image that requires adherence to general rules. To this puzzle there are several solutions. One of these originates with Freud, who sees in the sense of duty an internalization of parental and social commands, pride in their observance being due to a conscious or unconscious equation of worth with obedience to authority. Another solution is best exemplified by Kant, although such un-Kantian figures as Nietzsche and Gabriel Marcel have also subscribed to it. According to these thinkers a man feels bound to general rules because he has freely chosen them or committed himself to them and because a failure to observe them would be tantamount to a betrayal of his own freely chosen personal identity. Still a third solution, in some respects allied to the foregoing, has been proposed by Jean Piaget, who sees a mature sense of duty as a product of two sources: (a) social activities such as childhood and adolescent games in which individuals functioning jointly as a group create rules and bind themselves to these rules of their own creation, and (b) a mental development in which the individual acquires working familiarity with the concepts of law, universality, noncontradiction, and other logical or scientific principles.[5]

Freud's solution, though undoubtedly reductionistic, no less undoubtedly contains elements of truth; for there can be no question either that the content of the rules that the sense of duty commands us to observe is most often derived from social sources or that the sense of self-esteem is with most persons closely related to the esteem accorded them by others. What this solution fails to explain is how, as in the case of many a social or moral reformer, the content of moral rules deviates from socially accepted practice and how the individual feels bound to revolt against external authority in order to preserve his self-esteem. The second solution, though in large part designed to answer this very problem, does not give full satisfaction. As Nietzsche says, man alone among the animals makes promises, to himself or to others, and unquestionably the sense of self-esteem does often depend upon our capacity for personal commitment to rules. But this solution gives no hint as to why some individuals can abandon self-imposed commitments with relatively little distress whereas others cannot—which is precisely what most urgently needs to be explained.

Fortunately, Piaget's solution makes up in great part for the deficiencies of both other theories. The statistical data he has collected show a strong positive correlation between the mature sense of moral duty on the one hand and the development of logicality and participation in activities requiring adherence to mutually agreed upon rules on the other. In itself, of course, the correlation means little, but when interpreted in the light of a few elementary psychological facts the correlation is seen to be more than accidental. As Piaget points out, a theory like Freud's is perfectly adequate to account for the sense of duty of small children, as well as of many immature adults. For them, moral rules are to be observed because they are externally commanded and because one will be punished by external agents for not observing them. But

[5] See especially Jean Piaget, *The Moral Judgment of the Child,* trans. Gabain (Glencoe: The Free Press, 1948).

it is not true that when the typical child has reached that stage in his development where moral rules are no longer regarded as externally imposed, he has simply internalized parental or other adult precepts. The difference between child and adult is too enormous to permit identification, and without identification there can be no internalization. What happens is that the child who participates in group activities at school or on the playground has at last found a peer group—a group composed of members sufficiently like himself in strength and knowledge and interests that identification becomes possible. Then and only then does the child feel that he has entered a moral community as a free agent; then and only then does the child feel committed to rules because of an individual choice that he cannot renounce without renouncing his personal identity.

So far so good. Piaget has successfully avoided the vagueness of Kant and the reductionism of Freud with respect to the manner in which an individual comes to feel that his self-esteem and personal identity depend upon commitment to rule. But how can Piaget explain that the individual frequently rejects the rules of the group as a matter of duty and in order to preserve his self-esteem? Although Piaget himself apparently did not fully appreciate this, the empirical correlations he established do help us to explain the moral or social reformer. Let me begin by observing that the reformer does not create his rules out of thin air. Few if any reformers have ever demanded more than a re-examination of subsidiary moral standards in the light of more basic standards. The moral reformer is primarily a man whose intellectual conscience is sufficiently developed that he is aware of inconsistencies among the many socially given moral rules and unable to tolerate them. What he calls for is moral coherence and a more appropriate adjustment of means to basic aims. As remarked in the last chapter, conservatives tend to deprecate reason whereas radicals and liberals most often fall into the class of intellectuals. While conservatives respond globally to the entire complex of existing social values and standards, unwilling or unable to distinguish means from ends and unwilling or unable to respond discriminatingly to the relative values of the many standards within the total complex, the liberal sifts, compares, and evaluates each, often organizing them in hierarchical fashion, rejecting whatever has no logical place within his scheme. The liberal is frequently in the unenviable position of having to free himself from emotional attachment to a moral rule that fails to fit the logical pattern, as well as having to face general social opposition; but his demand for consistency permits him no other course, and, fortunately, the satisfaction of being true to himself often compensates him. As Socrates said,

> I would rather that my lyre should be inharmonious, and that there should be no music in the chorus which I provided; aye, or that the whole world should be at odds with me, and oppose me, rather than that I myself should be at odds with myself, and contradict myself.[6]

It is, therefore, by no means surprising that a correlation between a developed sense of duty and the awareness of logical principles should go together. Nor is it surprising that both should correlate with participation in peer-group activities such as games, for nothing is more essential to the successful practice of games or any other organized social activity than a consistent set of rules.

Although the spirit of benevolence and the sense of duty are clearly distinct phenomena and on occasion even dispose us to behave differently in the same situation, they do normally work together along with crude self-interest, a man being honest or generous from all three motives. However, the spirit of benevolence and the sense of duty are each subject to forms of distortion and over-development for which the other is the most satisfactory and reliable corrective. No noncognitive factor is more valuable in assuring us that the content of the rules to which a man feels bound through the sense of duty will be socially desirable than the spirit of benevolence; and nothing is more valuable in extending the individual's range of moral concern, too often limited to narrow circles, than the sense of duty. It may be

[6] *The Dialogues of Plato,* trans. Jowett (New York: Random House, Inc., 1937), V. II, p. 542.

relevant to point out here the common belief that men, whose greater participation in social life and superior education dispose them to relatively greater moral idealism than women, are also more prone to a rigidly moralistic approach to life; whereas women, who often get more loving attention than men and of whom society demands less in the way of logicality, are more likely to abandon moral scruple in the defense of family and friend.

In summary, then, my position is that the three greatest noncognitive factors in the development of moral character are self-love, the spirit of benevolence, and the sense of duty. Self-love is a natural tendency of the human animal, whereas the spirit of benevolence and the sense of duty are social products, but to direct the former into socially acceptable channels and to create the latter much more is required than moral exhortation. Ultimately the moral health of the individual depends upon the collective wisdom of society, which is itself dependent upon a widespread and co-operative practice of rationality in all spheres of life—political and economic no less than narrowly educational.

chapter seven

FREEDOM, SELFHOOD, AND MORAL RESPONSIBILITY

By a chain of inferences, each of them appearing at first sight irrefutable, one easily arrives at a conclusion that strikes at the heart of my position. If, it is said, an individual is morally responsible for an act, that act must be performed freely; if the act is performed freely, the individual must himself be its author; and if the individual is himself its author, then the act can be causally explained neither in terms of external circumstances nor in terms of biological inheritance. In other words, to the extent that the individual is a morally responsible agent, he is free; and to the extent that he is free, he transcends the biological, physical, and social conditions of his being. Consequently my position must be false. It cannot be that the moral development of the individual is largely a matter of social circumstance, nor can it be that the individual's primary moral responsibility is to add to the sum of human well-being. The autonomy of the free moral agent is a gift of God which transports him into the society of angels—not a natural debt which the individual must discharge in the mundane world of human affairs. In this chapter I shall try to show that this argument, despite its initial plausibility, rests upon highly dubious assumptions about the nature of the moral self and of human freedom. I shall also try to show how a proper understanding of moral selfhood and freedom confirms my own views. Freedom is not only compatible with determinism, it is a product of determinism.

LIBERTARIANISM

The essence of libertinism, as the position against which I am arguing is ordinarily called, is not that a free act is totally uncaused or undetermined, although critics of libertarianism frequently tend to give this impression. The essence of the position is rather that the moral self is an autonomous being that chooses or generates its own values and that in tracing the causal antecedents of a free act one must come to a full stop when one finally encounters this autonomous activity of the moral self. The most famous as well as the most able of the libertarians are Immanuel Kant and Jean-Paul Sartre. Kant refers to the moral agent as a self-legislating *noumenal* self independent of external influences and opposes it to the empirical, or phenomenal, self, the latter a creature of desire and passion that *is* subject to determination by external influences. The noumenal self issues moral commands; it is for the phenomenal self to obey. Sartre dispenses with the concept of the noumenal self, arguing that the individual as moral agent is a pure nothingness that spontaneously manifests itself by directly creating its empirical, or phenomenal, needs and desires.

Against the libertarian view of selfhood and freedom, whether Kantian or Sartrean, I have three principal objections.

1. It is extremely difficult to conceive at all concretely the libertarian self and at least as difficult to establish its actual existence. Kant freely admits that we have no knowledge of the noumenal self and that its existence is simply a postulate that he believes necessary to the moral life. At best it might be said that the noumenal self is an hypothesis needed to explain that elementary and actually observable fact of moral experience, the conflict between duty and desire. As I have already shown in Chapter II, however, the conflict between duty and desire can be quite adequately explained without recourse to any unobservable entities of this kind. Sartre, for his part, claims that our existence as a nothingness that spontaneously chooses its own values

can be established through an intuitive insight coming to us in the experience of anguish. But knowledge revealed in this manner is no more reliable than knowledge revealed to the religious mystic, and if we accept such alleged insights as valid we shall have almost as many different accounts of the nature of the self as there are persons who claim to know the self in this way.

2. Both the Kantian and the Sartrean views of moral selfhood raise problems to which no satisfactory answer appears forthcoming. Kant, for instance, must explain how the noumenal self actually influences the conduct of the phenomenal self, since most of us subscribe to the Spinozistic view that a desire can be combatted only with the aid of another desire and do not, therefore, see how a command issued by an affectless noumenal self can by itself counteract such phenomenal affects as self-love. Kant would sometimes have us understand that this takes place through the intermediary of "the will." But nowhere does he clearly describe the will. What is it? Is it an empirical phenomenon? If so, why is its existence so widely contested, especially by empirical psychologists? Or is it a nonempirical phenomenon whose existence Kant merely postulates along with the noumenal self? If so, the problem has been displaced, not solved. Sartre's problem is to explain how our empirical desires correlate so consistently with other empirical facts, especially social circumstances. If our concrete desires were manifestations of a purely spontaneous choice by ourselves as nonempirical agents, then it would certainly seem that predictions based upon empirical correlations between felt desires or character traits, on the one hand, and natural or social circumstances, on the other, would be altogether unreliable—which is contrary to fact.

3. Finally, libertarian selfhood and freedom, even if they were *vera causa,* could not possibly be an adequate explanation of moral responsibility for two distinct but related reasons.

a. To say that a person is morally responsible for an act is to say that he may properly be praised or blamed by other persons for that act. But it is generally agreed that a person may not properly be praised or blamed for his past or present behavior and cannot consequently be held morally responsible for it unless there is reason to believe that praise or blame is likely to have some effect upon his future behavior. If, for instance, we believed that a man were drinking to excess and that moral censure by a well-disposed friend might have the effect of curbing overindulgence in the future, we would in all probability recognize the legitimacy of moral censure. If, however, we were convinced that the man's drinking had reached the stage where moral censure would be totally ineffective, as it would be if his drinking were thoroughly compulsive, we would almost certainly consider the use of moral censure improper. In this latter case the man would cease to be an agent in the proper sense of that term, *viz.*, a person who acts of his own volition. He would be instead a patient, someone acted upon by circumstances over which he has no control. To censure him would be a useless act of cruelty. The point is that no matter how wrong an act may be considered objectively in terms of its consequences for the well-being of the person involved or for the well-being of others, an act is not wrong in the sense that it may properly elicit blame unless blame will serve a useful purpose. Similarly, we do not proportion the praise that a man receives simply to the moral value of his behavior as judged by its consequences. Let us say that two men have performed acts of kindness of equal objective value but that whereas the first of these men is known to have previously performed few acts of kindness, the second is known to have performed many such acts. Surely it is the first who will receive the warmest accolades. Here again the explanation is that we regard it as improper to distribute praise and blame without taking into account the effect it is likely to have upon the future conduct of the persons concerned, and it is clear that the probable effect of praise upon the first man's future conduct would be greater than upon that of the second man, whose generous dispositions are already deeply entrenched. Now, if so much is granted, what follows with respect to the contention that a man cannot be held morally responsible for his behavior unless it is free in the sense that it has not been determined by external circumstances? Clearly that contention will have to be rejected. The foregoing argument implies that to be morally responsible the individual's behavior must be subject to determination by moral suasion from other persons, *i.e.,* by external causal factors.

b. It is generally agreed that we cannot hold an individual morally responsible for his behavior unless we know the empirical circumstances of his behavior. Killing, for instance, is wrong when considered objectively in terms of its consequences. But before praising or blaming a man for a particular act of killing we must know the concrete circumstances. Was it in self-defense, for the sake of gain, in the line of duty, etc.? Now, what could be clearer than that in determining the circumstances of an individual's behavior we treat them as partial causes? Once again we see that causality by external circumstances, far from being a reason for withholding ascriptions of moral responsibility, is, in fact, a necessary condition of such ascriptions.

FREEDOM AND MORAL RESPONSIBILITY

Nothing in the preceding section was intended to suggest that "freedom" and "moral selfhood" are empty terms. What I disputed was merely one, almost exclusively philosophical, use of these expressions—a use that I believe to be not only irrelevant to moral experience but also far removed from the meaning that these terms are usually given and by right ought to be given in actual moral discourse. As will be seen, the terms "freedom" and "moral responsibility" have two distinguishable popular uses. One of the popular uses of the term "freedom" is directly related to the use of the term "moral responsibility" when the latter is employed neutrally to signify legitimate liability to praise or blame. The other—and larger—use of the term "freedom" is less directly related to "moral responsibility" so defined; its proper correlate is the honorific use of the term "moral responsibility," as when we say that a man behaved in a thoroughly responsible way in the face of a very trying situation. In the present section, however, the term "moral responsibility" will be used in the neutral sense, as it has been up to this point, my first task being to analyze the meaning of the term "freedom" where freedom is said to be a necessary condition for ascriptions of praise or blame.

My contention is that freedom as a condition of moral responsibility implies with respect to any given act (a) that if an individual *chose* to perform it he could do so and (b) that deliberation could be causally efficacious in causing the individual to choose or not to choose to perform it. The import of (a) and (b) can best be seen by considering what each excludes from the sphere of free behavior. By (a) we see that an individual's freedom is restricted by physical disability and by psychological compulsion. A cripple is obviously not free to walk. Nor is the hopeless alcoholic free to quit drinking, though typically he is free to choose or resolve to do so at frequent intervals. By (b) we see that an individual's freedom is restricted by personality traits so deeply rooted that he cannot seriously consider acting in a manner that runs counter to them. An example would be the man whose sense of duty or spirit of benevolence is so strong that no amount of reflection with regard to the advantages to be gained by betraying a friend or the hardships to be undergone as a consequence of remaining loyal could possibly have any bearing upon his choices. Another example would be the individual who is so thoroughly selfish that no considerations that might be brought to his attention would induce him to remain loyal to his associates if by acting otherwise he could reasonably expect private advantage.

It should be carefully noted that condition (b) is wholly distinct from condition (a). This is a point that can be easily overlooked, condition (b) often being assimilated to condition (a). The person whose freedom is restricted by condition (a) is someone who can choose to behave differently than he in fact does but who cannot execute his choice. The person whose freedom is restricted by condition (b), on the other hand, is someone who could execute a choice but who cannot make that choice. The difference between the two cases is that the man who suffers from a physical disability or who acts compulsively can be made to see and frequently does see that his actual behavior is undesirable; whereas the man who cannot be moved to choose otherwise than he does as a result of deliberation cannot be so moved precisely because it is impossible for him, given his character, actually to believe that behavior of a different kind would be desirable. For him there is no live option; he has no genuine alternatives. He can, of course, envisage the consequences of a different pattern of conduct, but that alternative pattern of conduct either makes no appeal to his affective nature or else arouses strong negative reactions.

Although (a) and (b) are both necessary conditions of moral responsibility, they do not even jointly constitute a sufficient condition. To be legitimately liable to praise or blame the act in question must also be determinable as right or wrong. This third condition of moral responsibility does not, however, play any role in our use of the term "freedom." When we say that freedom is a necessary condition of moral responsibility all that we normally mean, and all that we ought to mean, is that conditions (a) and (b) have both been met. If an individual has genuine alternatives between which deliberation might decide and if a choice made after deliberation could be executed, the individual is free in the requisite sense. And this is the case even though the individual's decision to deliberate, as well as the outcome of the deliberation, is wholly determined by his past experience and external circumstances. We do, of course, often and rightly withhold praise or blame when an individual's choice is known to be determined. But this is not *because* the choice was determined; it is because the determining factors are too powerful to be counteracted by moral sanctions. If, for instance, the conditions of a man's life have led him to choose a criminal career and also to respond with bitterness and hatred to moral censure, we would do well to withhold blame—not, however, because his choice was determined but because he has been determined to react negatively to blame. Besides, what difference can it make to us that a man's choices are wholly determined if our actions and his deliberations both figure among the possible determining factors? We do not live for the past; we live for the future. And to bend the future to our will we must rely upon causal laws.

It might be objected that if a man's behavior is wholly determined by his past experience and external circumstances, then he could not be free since freedom implies that he is the author of his behavior. But this objection cannot be allowed. If an individual's choices are among the causal antecedents of his behavior, then he *is* the author of that behavior. If B is the cause of C, B remains the cause of C even though A is the cause of B. If a man is led to deliberate and to act differently than he would otherwise have done because of our intervention, his behavior must none the less be credited to him. Similarly, if because of favorable childhood experiences a man is extraordinarily benevolent, it is none the less he who is benevolent. The real threat to the moral dignity of the individual is not determinism, but determination by factors that develop weak or morally deficient personalities instead of strong and morally wholesome ones.

Some libertarians will also object because in my definition of freedom I have omitted any reference to the will. In considering the question of the will, let us picture a man who, though not a confirmed alcoholic, is in danger of becoming one. This man is aware that his drinking causes hardship to his family and embarrassment to his friends, and these are facts to which he is not indifferent. He also suffers from a loss of self-esteem and is disturbed by the adverse judgments of others. However, he finds it difficult to get through a normal workday of difficult business conferences without a substantial number of drinks. He dreads going home to a nagging wife and querulous children. He enjoys the warm camaraderie of old friends from college days who regularly get together for drinks at the end of the day. And spending big sums in public places helps satisfy his ego drives. This man is thus torn between the specifically moral motives of benevolence, duty, and desire for moral approval that incline him to abandon drinking and a set of motives without special moral relevance that dispose him to continue. Now, according to most libertarians a favorable outcome of this struggle will depend largely upon the strength of the man's will. According to my view a favorable resolution will depend largely upon rational discipline, especially the accuracy and concreteness with which the individual analyzes the motives at work and represents to himself the consequences of the possible courses of conduct open to him.

As already stated, I reject the notion of will because I am unaware of any evidence for the existence of anything corresponding to it. I also reject the concept because no one to my knowledge has ever offered a satisfactory criterion by which it can be decided whether a man who succumbs to temptation has done so through weakness of will or as a result of the strength of the temptation. Moreover, it is very difficult to see how anyone *could* provide a satisfactory criterion. I ask the reader to imagine that the man in the example given becomes a hopeless alcoholic. How would you even go about deciding whether he was overcome by psychological forces and external circumstances beyond his control or whether he was simply weak-willed? I do not, of course, claim that it would always be easy to determine whether such a man fell prey to the compulsion of drink because of a failure properly to deliberate, but certainly this is a far less forbidding task. And certainly there is more reason to hope that moral suasion would lead the man to an accurate appraisal of his situation and consequently to a desirable resolution of his problem than to hope that moral suasion would produce a movement of this dubious entity called the will. That deliberation could bring into play what we have called the moral motives and cause these motives to prevail over others can be easily understood; for motives usually operate only when we believe that the circumstances are appropriate, and it is by deliberation that we decide what the circumstances are. How the will could bring the moral motives into play is for me a mystery.

It might be countered that I have misrepresented the libertarian position and falsely located the problem. The libertarian view, it might be said, is not so irrationalist as suggested, for libertarians do recognize that reason must decide how the individual ought to behave. And the problem is not to determine how the will brings moral motives into play, but how the will implements rational choice. Assume, for instance, that the man in our example has decided that the right thing to do is to quit drinking. Suppose further that, though he has decided to quit drinking, the empirical moral motives—the sense of duty, benevolence, and the desire for approval—are still weaker than the nonmoral motives. How is he to execute his decision? It is to explain that men do frequently execute decisions under circumstances like these, so the objection continues, that the notion of the will was invoked. I will not quarrel with this interpretation of libertarianism; some libertarians do hold this position. But I will quarrel with the contention that a rational decision about right behavior ever does cause us to act unless it enlists the support of empirical motives.

To say, for instance, that the incipient alcoholic has decided that the right thing for him to do is to quit drinking could only mean that he has come to believe one or some combination of four things: (a) that it is in his best interests to quit, (b) that to quit is to act in accordance with a moral rule, (c) that to quit is beneficial to others, or (d) that not quitting will lead to moral disapproval. If (a) is the basis of the decision then there is no problem as to how it is translated into action. If (b) is the basis of the decision, it will be effective only if the individual has actually committed himself to the rule and would suffer loss of self-esteem by not observing it. If (c) is the basis of the decision, it will be translated into action only to the extent that the individual actually cares about the welfare of others. If, finally, (d) is the basis, the decision will result in action only to the extent that the individual in fact fears moral disapproval.

Of course, the generalizations about human motivation that I have just offered cannot be proved in any strict sense. Nor can I in any strict sense of the term prove that the person who claims to introspect an entity properly called will, which sometimes tips the scales in favor of right and reason, is wrong. I can only say that for myself I have never been able to introspect in any instance of moral struggle elements other than those indicated here, nor have I felt the need to introduce additional elements to account for the moral behavior of others.

There is still another objection to my position that I feel called upon to answer, and once again I find it advisable to state that objection with reference to a concrete example. Suppose that a man were required to betray another person or else submit to torture and possible death. Now, consistently with the position I have just outlined this man would not be subject to praise for submitting to torture and possible death if one of his moral motives, such as the sense of duty, were so strongly developed that the other possibility was not for him a genuine alternative. Similarly, a man would not be subject to blame for betraying his friend under these circumstances if his moral motives were so weakly developed that self-love would necessarily prevail. Moreover, if moral motives inclining him to abstain were genuinely competitive with other motives inclining him to betray, then consistent with the thesis maintained in Chapter I the individual probably ought in deliberating to give full weight to all motives concerned and finally to act after having decided what constitutes his own best long-range interests. The pertinent point in this third case is that in deliberating men can, and no doubt some men do, dwell more or less exclusively upon motives inclining them to act according to their ideas of moral right, shutting out of mind considerations that tend to bring other motives into play. According to the view maintained in this book, however, to do so would be not only irrational but in all likelihood morally wrong. Can anyone, so the objection goes, seriously maintain such utterly paradoxical theses?

Now, it will not be gainsaid that my position with respect to these three cases has an air of paradox. Intellectually, we are all natural conservatives; old and familiar views die hard. None the less, however paradoxical these views may seem, we cannot logically reject them without embracing views that are even more paradoxical.

Consider the first case. A man has submitted to torture and possible death rather than betray another person. By hypothesis his motive was a strongly developed sense of duty—a sense of duty so strongly developed that no matter how long or how concretely he fixed in mind the advantages of acting differently he would not be able to do so. Why is he not legitimately to be praised? Because, I answer, he was not free to act otherwise than he did; because as he himself would be the first to tell us he had no choice in the matter; and because praise for this act would be as little likely to affect his behavior in similar future situations as blame would be likely to cure the confirmed dope addict. One could not consistently maintain that this man ought to be praised without at the same time denying that freedom is a necessary condition of moral responsibility and affirming that moral approval ought to be expressed even though it cannot serve a useful purpose.

The air of paradox in the position I have adopted will be further dispelled if we bear in mind the following points: (1) Although this man cannot be legitimately praised, he can be admired. For the same reasons that admiration rather than praise is appropriate with respect to physical beauty or native intelligence, so admiration rather than praise is appropriate with respect to established moral traits that have become second nature. (2) Although praise is something that almost all men covet, praise from one's moral inferiors is a matter of relative indifference and under many circumstances may properly be regarded as presumptuous. To praise another man implies that one is, if not his moral superior, at least his moral equal. And how many of us are the moral equal of our hypothetical hero? (3) There is something highly artificial about this hypothetical case. To simplify the argument I assumed that the sole motive operating in favor of the hero's actual behavior was a sense of duty and that it was so strongly developed that of itself it guaranteed a desirable outcome. In fact, however, it is almost always the case, even where we are witness to the most exalted moral fervor, that many motives are at work and that few of them are so strong that they could not conceivably be reinforced by praise. My criterion for deciding when praise is due will not, therefore, exclude many cases in which a man has acted nobly.

Consider the second case. A man has betrayed another rather than submit to torture and possible death himself. By hypothesis his motives were selfish, the moral motives being too weak effectively to compete even though they all are given due consideration. Why is this man not to be legitimately blamed? Again, the answer is: because he was not free to act differently than he did; because, though not compelled to act as he did, he was none the less constrained to choose as he did; and because blame would be useless. It might be objected here that blame would not be useless. The moral motives include not only the sense of duty and the spirit of benevolence but also the fear of social disapprobation, and by blaming the man we might actually influence the balance of factors determining his behavior. But this objection rests upon the false assumption that we blame people for their behavior before they have acted. It is true that before acting the man will if he chooses rationally make a fair estimate of the amount of disapprobation he is likely to encounter as a result of his behavior. But the crucial factor here is not the disapprobation that actually follows; the crucial factor is his *estimate* of the disapprobation that is likely to ensue, and this estimate can only be based upon generalizations from past experience.

I would be quite willing to rest my argument on the points just made; but, as before, I shall adduce a few considerations that may help to overcome resistance. (1) Although we are not entitled to blame this man, we are entitled to feel offended by the baseness of his character. Physical ugliness offends the eye, and the man who is not offended by it no doubt lacks aesthetic sensibility. Similarly, moral ugliness offends persons of moral character. But to blame a man for moral ugliness that cannot be corrected by blame is as useless and cruel as to blame a man who has had the misfortune of being born with three eyes and two noses. (2) To blame a man generally implies that the most effective cause of his behavior lies within him and that the most effective remedy is effort on his part; but in cases of the kind illustrated by this example these implications are false, and by blaming the agent we simply divert attention from the true cause and true remedy. The true cause in the illustrative example is this man's living in a society where individuals have not been given adequate moral training and where they can be terrorized into performing base acts. The true remedy is social action. An analogy may make this clearer. Someone, noting comparative statistics on homicide, illegitimacy, venereal disease, absenteeism from work, desertions from military forces, etc., may issue a moral condemnation of the Negro race. To do so is clearly to give a false impression about the effective causes of the moral weaknesses to which these statistics point and to discourage efforts to eliminate discrimination. (3) Finally, as noted above, the motives of our behavior are usually far more complex than in the hypothetical cases we are considering; and since among them there are almost always some that might be favorably altered by moral censure the person with an incurable itch to blame his fellow men for wrong-doing will not be so sorely frustrated if he adopts my criterion for the distribution of blame as he might at first sight suppose.

Consider now the third case, that of the man who has a genuine choice between the two possible lines of conduct, who can by guiding the course of deliberation and dwelling more or less exclusively upon the advantages of acting in accord with the established moral rules persuade himself to choose "rightly" but whose best interests when all relevant factors are considered require that he act "wrongly." My thesis is that this man ought not to be blamed for acting "wrongly." The probability is that it would be socially desirable if he were to be guided by rational appraisal of his best interests even though his best interests required him to violate established moral rule and even though he was free to follow them. Now, it is not my intention to repeat the whole of Chapter I, the principal object of which was to defend this very thesis. It will, however, be worthwhile briefly to restate and in some respects to elaborate upon the arguments of that chapter with the example that presently concerns us in mind.

1. A reasonably well-ordered moral society is one in which care has been taken to instill in its members a spirit of benevolence and a sense of duty and in which there prevails a system of rewards and punishments, including moral as well as economic and penal sanctions, such that most individuals will find it in their best interests to observe the established moral rules in most cases. This is in fact the kind of society we live in, and in a society of this kind the consistent practice of rationality as we defined it in Chapter IV will have a generally beneficial effect, since wrong-doing defined in terms of violation of conventional moral rules will normally be due to ignorance of true self-interest. The question then is whether we ought to encourage others to desist from

the practice of rationality in those special cases where they have good reason to believe that it will dispose them to violate established moral rules. My answer is that we ought not to do so. And the first of my three reasons is that rationality consists of a set of habitual dispositions that must be strengthened through practice and that will be weakened to the extent that they are violated. My point here is similar to one that could no doubt be used against me. I am in effect saying that a general rule of conduct that has proved its worth ought to be observed even in cases where it does not have its normal consequences, since by authorizing exceptions we tend to bring the rule into disrepute and to weaken a valuable habitual disposition. This line of reasoning has been used by moral philosophers for approximately twenty-five centuries in support of consistent observance of such moral rules as truth-telling and promise-keeping—rules of conduct that I insist the individual be permitted to violate without censure in those special cases where he has rationally determined that they are contrary to his true over-all interests. Note, however, that if my reasoning is correct, the rational pursuit of self-interest is a higher-order rule than rules of truth-telling, promise-keeping, etc., in the sense that the rule applies to a wider range of conduct and that action based upon it has on the whole more advantageous consequences. Also bear in mind the generally established principle that where a higher-order rule conflicts with lower-order rules, the higher-order rule ought to prevail.

Fortunately for society, persons with a strongly developed sense of duty or spirit of benevolence will rarely find themselves in situations where the higher-order rule dictating rational pursuit of self-interest conflicts with lower-order rules. The person with a strong sense of duty has chosen to realize his personal well-being by consistent adherence to lower-order rules and will suffer in self-esteem if he violates them. Violations are not, therefore, likely to be in his own interests. Similarly, since the person with a strong spirit of benevolence will be personally distressed by the thought of possible suffering to others attending violation of lower-order rules, self-interest itself will usually require that he observe them. Conflicts of the kind that we are discussing arise most frequently only when the sense of duty or spirit of benevolence is absent or very poorly developed, and in these cases the only effective instrument of social control is the use of sanctions appealing to the individual's self-love. If, however, we fail consistently to encourage rational pursuit of self-interest, the effectiveness of this one remaining instrument of social control will be impaired.

2. As pointed out in Chapter I and again in discussing the case of the man who was not free not to betray, to blame someone for his behavior is to imply that he is chiefly responsible for it and that the most effective remedy is largely within his personal power. Where, however, a man finds it in his interests to betray another, I do not believe that he is chiefly responsible or that corrective action on his part is very likely to be of avail. The chief culprit would be society and the most effective means of preventing further violations would be concerted social action. To blame individuals in cases of this kind is to perpetuate that sharp distinction between personal morality and social policy and to encourage that baseless optimism with respect to the value of mere moralizing that have been the bane of the Christian era in Western civilization.

3. By blaming a man for acting contrary to his best interests we shall either embitter him if he believes that blame is unjustified or else implant a disrespect for rationality and an unwholesome sense of guilt if he believes that it is justified. In either case we have deprived ourselves of whatever help the individual might otherwise have been able to offer in creating a better and happier society. That blame will embitter an offender of the established code if he believes it unjustified will probably not be disputed. My reasons for fearing disrespect for rationality if the individual is made to believe in the legitimacy of blame in these circumstances were presented in Chapter I and will not be repeated. It will, however, probably be asked why the sense of guilt over acting contrary to one's best interests is unwholesome. I reply that the sense of guilt is unwholesome unless its ultimate effect is to strengthen or enrich the individual's personality, thereby giving him cause for legitimate pride in the future, and that feelings of

guilt under the circumstances described cannot be expected to have this effect. It is true that feelings of guilt under these circumstances could lead the individual to act in the future so as to win greater respect from others and that the sense of self-worth in fact often depends upon the respect of others. But legitimate pride, the warranted sense of our own worth, does not depend upon the attitudes of others. No thoroughly self-respecting, autonomous moral agent will feel guilty simply because others disapprove of him, however unhappy or displeased he may be over their disapprobation. A genuine sense of worth derives exclusively from the individual's personal conviction that he has acted rightly and from the active exercise of his native capacities with the feeling of self-expansion and power that accompanies it.

These last observations bring me to the problem of the moral self and freedom in that larger sense of which I spoke at the beginning of this section.

FREEDOM AND MORAL SELFHOOD

When we say that an individual is not morally responsible for his behavior unless *he* is the author of that behavior, what do we mean by the word "he"? It is clear that we do not mean the physical self, and upon reflection it becomes equally clear that we do not mean the totality of the psychological self. An individual who is motivated by instinct is not to that extent the moral author of his behavior, nor is the man who acts from habit, desire, or impulse. Instincts, habits, desires, and impulses are no doubt properties of individuals, parts of their psychological make-up that must be included in any adequate description of their several selves. But the moral self, the self as an agent, as a causal factor in the genesis of behavior that may properly be called free, cannot be equated with the whole of the psychological self. This is not only because the moral self exercises a certain power over many of these motivational factors but also because the moral self is a higher self, a source of dignity and worth that cannot be ascribed to these other elements in our make-up. This does not mean, however, that the moral self must be regarded as a nothingness or as a transcendent, noumenal reality. The inadequacy of these conceptions has already been shown. What it means is that the moral self will have to be regarded as a limited aspect of the total psychological self. What aspect?

It would be tempting to answer that the moral self is identical with the moral motives, especially the spirit of benevolence and the sense of duty. I have myself suggested that an individual does not have great moral stature unless these motives are highly developed. Yet this answer will not do. If the moral self were defined in this way, then we could not appeal to the higher selves of persons in whom these motives remain undeveloped or regard these persons as moral agents—which in fact we do. Furthermore the moral motives themselves require guidance and direction by a moral agent. The moral self, the higher self, the self as agent can only be defined as the rational self: that ensemble of capacities, disciplines, and habitual dispositions that permits us to arbitrate among competing desires or other empirical motives and to achieve our chosen goals. We are morally responsible agents only to the extent that deliberation or forethought is capable of influencing choice and that choices once made can be successfully implemented.

But here a distinction is in order. The possession of rational capacities marks man as superior to the beasts, and it is to this that his existence as a free and morally responsible moral agent must be attributed. But there is a difference between the man who rightly exercises those capacities and the man who does not. Although in one sense of these terms a man is free and morally responsible simply because he possesses these capacities and regardless of how he uses them, in another sense of these terms he is free and morally responsible only if he actually uses them and, moreover, uses them rightly. Hitler, for instance, was a moral agent; he was substantially free in that much of his behavior was or could have been a consequence of deliberation; and he was morally responsible in that for many of his actions he could not properly have claimed exemption from blame. But it is most unlikely that he was free and morally responsible in the sense of these terms I am about to explicate.

When in any ordinary nonmoral context a man says that he is free to do something, he does of course mean that if he chooses to do it, he will be able to do it. To the extent that a man cannot achieve a chosen goal, he is frustrated by external obstacles or in bondage to his ignorance of the means by which these obstacles may be overcome. He also means that he is free to choose, that deliberation or reflection might influence his decision, that there are for him genuine alternatives. We are obviously not free to follow a course of action that we can only envisage with an invincible and overpowering distaste. But he means more than these two things. He means that it lies within his power to reconcile or harmonize conflicting desires so as to take the sting out of choice; for to the extent that a man cannot reconcile or harmonize his desires—as opposed to merely being able to choose between them—he is burdened with a nasty problem of choice, and whatever choice he finally makes will be more or less unsatisfactory.

"I am free to go to Europe," for instance, means that if I apply for a passport, ask for a vacation from work, attempt to purchase a ticket, etc., the passport will be granted, my employer will give me the necessary vacation time, the travel bureau will give me a reservation, etc. If I cannot persuade the State Department to give me a passport or my employer to give me a vacation, if it is a busy tourist season and I cannot book passage, etc., then I am not free to go to Europe. "I am free to go to Europe" also means that I can conceive of not going and that deliberation might have a bearing upon my choice. But, in addition, it means that I have found a way of harmonizing the desire to go to Europe with the main body of my other desires and that the satisfaction of this desire does not involve agonizing and painful sacrifices.

In this larger sense of the term no one, of course, is ever fully free. Few of us make major choices that do not involve painful sacrifice; and in ordinary discourse we accommodate ourselves to this fact of life, saying simply in a given situation that we are free, although strictly speaking we are only partially free. None the less it is evident that freedom as an ideal toward which we strive involves a measure of ease and psychological comfort, as well as the ability to choose and to act as we choose. And it is no less evident that the exercise of rationality is the principal condition of whatever measure of freedom we actually possess. This is not only because the rational man is better equipped than the nonrational man to make the best possible choice in any given situation and to overcome external obstacles but also because the rational man is better equipped satisfactorily to resolve internal conflicts and to harmonize competing desires. I repeat, however, that no man is wholly free and that the individual practice of rationality cannot guarantee even a relatively high measure of freedom. There are adverse environmental circumstances that would defeat even the most rational of us, and there are persons suffering from inner conflicts caused by early experiences that the most persistent rational effort will fail fully to resolve. Individual rational discipline will be an adequate guarantee of individual freedom only if and when society at large becomes a community of rational men.

Let us now inquire into the honorific meaning of moral responsibility. In praising a man for being morally responsible we do not necessarily imply that his behavior conforms to the accepted moral rules. There are, after all, morally responsible persons who not only violate some of the accepted moral rules but who do so from a sense of duty. Neither do we mean merely that the man has a strongly developed sense of duty or spirit of benevolence. The man who does not possess these traits may be morally responsible within certain limits, and even the man who possesses them must, if he is to be fully responsible, guide and direct them. To praise a man for his moral responsibility is fundamentally to declare that he is guided by reason, that he is a true agent who acts only after proper reflection and who can be trusted to act according to rational choice. The difference between moral responsibility in the restricted sense implying merely liability to praise or blame and moral responsibility in the larger and honorific sense lies wholly in the fact that the latter entails more than the former, *viz., rational* deliberation as opposed to simple capacity for deliberation. To be subject to moral sanctions it suffices that one be capable of deliberation, but a fully responsible moral agent must actually exercise that capability and exercise it rightly. The parallel between freedom in the large sense of the term and moral responsibility in the honorific sense is in this respect complete.

The upshot of the argument in this section is, then, that where freedom is regarded as the ultimate ideal of human striving and where moral responsibility is regarded as a singular token of high human achievement, the exercise of rationality is a condition of both. Whereas, however, freedom is the reward of rationality, moral responsibility is its price. The practice of rationality gives us power, and power is often a burden as well as a privilege. No one is so likely to be subject to moral censure by the voice of his conscience as the rational man, for no one is so conscious of the consequences of his acts, for evil as for good. And no one is so likely to be subjected to moral censure by his fellow man, for no one is more inclined to be impatient with popular prejudice and intellectual sloth. Should he withdraw into himself, he is the prey of his conscience; should he disturb the quiet sleep of his fellows, he must fight their resentment. The rational man lives not by a code that society has bequeathed him, but by a code which he has forged in the heat of intense personal experience. He knows the exacting demands of reflection, the torment of not being able always to justify his behavior, the pain of having to let go of comfortable prejudices, the suspicion of many natural impulses, the sometimes desperate need to articulate, and the stubborn, often willful, incomprehension of others. But he does not lead a dull and colorless life of quiet desperation; he does not trade dignity for security; and when he collapses, if he does, it is not through personal weakness. Like Socrates, Spinoza, Marx, and Freud, he knows the joys of creativity, and, feeling the weight of his own self, he cannot be indifferent to the potentialities of other human personalities. He will not, therefore, cynically exploit other persons' weaknesses nor sentimentally minister to their prejudices. He abhors all that cheapens human contacts, reducing human beings to tools for the satisfaction of one another's sordid needs for security, social privilege, professional advancement, or mere escape from neurotic loneliness. And if he is contemptuous of others, his contempt springs less from a sense of personal superiority than from the exhilarating awareness of what it would be like were human relationships based upon the sense of personal dignity and inner strength that can only be purchased through the exercise of reason.

There are, of course, especially in this age of maudlin sentimentality and irresponsible flight from freedom, those who would rather be pitied than blamed and who would rather that their adult behavior be determined by early toilet training or external authorities than by mature, individual reflection. It must, however, be borne in mind that if moral responsibility is the fate of the strong, contempt is the fate of the weak. And it must also be borne in mind that the man who trades his dignity and individuality for security, eschewing the labor of rationality, more often than not strikes a bad bargain; the security that he purchases so dearly is a false security.

To be sure, selfhood is a difficult achievement, and, to be sure, a world without compassion and sympathy, a world in which the individual finds no support or guidance from the community, would be intolerable. But very often pity is an affront to human dignity, as many young social workers afire with the idea that *tout comprendre c'est tout pardonner* have soon discovered. Frequently blame is not only more appropriate but more welcome. And, as many a conformist has discovered to his chagrin, exclusive reliance upon the community has as its consequence, not the sense of solid well-being he had hoped to find, but merely an obliteration of his sense of personal identity. Spinoza once remarked that there are men who, having renounced their role as rational moral agents, are merely acted upon and that when they cease to be acted upon they cease to be. This remark is not strictly correct. These men cease to be, not when they cease to be acted upon, but from the moment they cease to act. For it is the distinguishing mark of a person as opposed to a beast that his very being lies in the exercise of his rational powers. The person as moral agent cannot be less than an autonomous rational being.

chapter eight

RELIGION AND ETHICS

Traditionally, religion has been related to ethics in two ways. On the one hand, men have appealed to religious authorities, ecclesiastical or scriptural, for instruction as to what ought to be done. On the other hand, they have resorted to religious belief as a source of moral energy. With respect to religion as a basis for a concrete moral code, very little will here be said. It is clear that we have no valid reason for obeying a divinely decreed moral code unless we have reason to believe in the goodness of the divinity who promulgated this code. His goodness must, however, be established on independent grounds. If there were no purely human morality, there would be no way of establishing the existence of a deity entitled to be called just or benevolent. This function of religion is thus no longer much stressed by philosophers and theologians, who have come more and more to recognize the hopeless circularity of any appeal to religious authority as a means of determining what ought to be done. This is so much so that A. Campbell Garnett, a leading Protestant philosopher, writes in *Religion and the Moral Life* that his book is

> a study of the relation between religious faith and the moral life. It agrees with both Catholic and Protestant theology that man's insight into the essential nature of his duty to his fellows is independent of his theological beliefs, but that his practical capacity to hold

> true to the highest ideals is vitally affected by the possession of a religious faith and by the quality of that faith.[1]

In the present chapter I shall investigate this latter claim. My conclusion will be that traditional religious views are on the whole inimical to the practice of morality.

First, however, I must say a few words about religion. In addition to the function already noted, religion is generally expected to serve two other purposes—that of reconciling the individual to the tragic aspects of life, i.e. providing him with consolation in times of distress, and that of explaining man's status within the total scheme of things or, as the existentialists put it, giving a satisfactory account of "the human condition." This is especially true of the great religions in the Western tradition. In fact, the major problems of traditional Western religious thought spring from the attempt simultaneously to satisfy these three demands. The problem of faith versus reason, for example, has its profound source in the attempt to give a rational account of the human condition that satisfies the need for consolation without undermining moral responsibility. As long as what we consider a rational account of man's status in the world serves these other functions we have no need of a nonrational faith and consequently no problem of faith versus reason. Similarly, the problem of reconciling grace and free will or of explaining how God's mercy relates to his justice arises because for purposes of hope and consolation God is construed as a merciful being who freely dispenses grace, whereas for the sake of maintaining the moral and social order he is construed as a perfectly just God who will impartially punish every infraction of moral rules. Reason, however, balks at simultaneously regarding the deity in both these ways.

I shall, therefore, define a religion as a set of beliefs designed to satisfy these three functions, and it will be well to point out at once that, given this definition, it becomes theoretically possible for naturalism to be regarded as a religion. And not only

[1] A. Campbell Garnett, *Religion and the Moral Life* (New York: Ronald Press, 1955), p. v.

theoretically! I shall, in fact, argue that naturalism is a superior religion in that it fulfills this triple function more adequately than traditional religious views.

THEISM

By "theism" I understand the popular Jewish, Christian, and Moslem belief in a personal creator who rewards the virtuous with eternal salvation and condemns the sinful to eternal torments in hell. I do not, of course, mean to suggest either that this is the whole of what those who call themselves theists would include in their articles of faith or that all men who call themselves theists would wholly agree with even this partial statement of their position. This definition does, however, approximate the core of theistic belief, and it will be helpful if at this stage we confine attention to this core of belief.

As an explanation of the human condition, theism is not very satisfactory. Although many theologians have attempted to prove one or another of the tenets of theism by argument, almost all admit that several tenets must be made to rest on faith, and some have even contended that no tenets can be rationally demonstrated. Moreover, the rationality of such arguments as have been offered is a matter of sharp dispute.

It would, no doubt, be rash to assert that men are incapable of genuine belief in propositions for which clear-cut rational evidence cannot be offered. Still, it is very probable that the belief of most persons who profess theism is less vital than religious leaders would like it to be. And for those who can accomplish the difficult feat of genuinely believing in theism, its consolatory power is usually slight. The fear of hell inclines as much to despair as the hope of eternal bliss inclines to consolation. It might be countered that despite the fear of damnation theism provides a sense of warmth and security insofar as God symbolizes paternal affection and disciplined authority. But this is to overlook the fact that a father symbol is as likely to be threatening as heart-warming. The sense of helplessness and fear is quite as often the dominant fact of childhood as the sense of warmth and security. Surely it cannot be denied that religious dread has been as prominent in historical Christendom as religious joy. It might also be said that despite the fear of damnation, theism, at least, offers man the hope of immortality. But if one were to judge on the basis of a comparison between theistic and nontheistic literature—and there is little else to go on—the fear of death appears to be actually greater among theists than among nontheists. The explanation of this curious fact may be, as Spinoza suggested, that fear feeds on hope and that when men are not bidden to believe in immortality, their meditation becomes a meditation on life rather than upon death. But whatever the explanation may be, the fear of death appears to be encouraged rather than allayed by theism.

The relationship between theism and morality is more complex. Theists attempt to support the view that religion disposes men to act morally in two ways. If, they say, men desire bliss and fear damnation and if they believe that they will be rewarded with bliss for virtue and damned for vice, then obviously they will have a greater tendency to act virtuously. And who can deny that theists do desire eternal bliss and do fear eternal damnation? This argument has a long ancestry, and many theists, especially Enlightenment thinkers like Voltaire and Franklin, have given it an even stronger statement, arguing that if men do not believe in a system of rewards and penalties after life they cannot be expected to be virtuous. Theism not only encourages virtuous behavior; it is a necessary condition of minimal virtue, especially among the lower classes. Now, there can be no question that self-love is a powerful motive, nor is it reasonable to question that men who do genuinely believe in rewards and punishments after death will, other things being equal, tend to be more virtuous than those who do not. But is there the slightest shred of evidence for the view that theism has ever had a sufficiently strong hold on the human imagination to have appreciably affected the behavior of any group of human beings? Is there any evidence, for instance, that atheistic soldiers are less brave than their theistic comrades, that the Greeks at Thermopylae, who did not believe in an after-life, were less brave than the Christian Crusaders? I am aware of none. Moreover, is there not something both morally repugnant and socially dangerous in the version of this argument offered by Voltaire and Franklin? If the belief in immortality is a necessary condition of morality, the logical conclusion is that all persons who are incapable of sustaining this belief will have to be excluded from the moral community. And the way is open to exclude them as well from the civil community, a step that John Locke actually recommended.

The second theistic argument that religion disposes men to act morally is that the image of God as a loving father tends to heighten consciousness of the brotherhood of men and thereby to encourage concern for general human well-being. To this argument I have two principal objections. (1) Theists have put the cart before the horse. The belief in God as a loving father does not encourage sentiments of benevolence. It is the spirit of benevolence that disposes men to believe in God as a loving father. And the spirit of benevolence, as I have shown in earlier chapters, is an outgrowth of early childhood circumstances with which religion has little or nothing to do. If the individual's childhood experiences are unfavorable, if his relationships to his earthly father are troubled, if there is rivalry between himself and other children for parental affection, an image of God as a loving father does not ordinarily emerge. (2) This argument assumes the existence of a link between the image of God as a loving father and the image of humankind as bound by ties of fraternity. It is doubtful whether this link actually exists. If the theistic image of the human condition is based psychologically on an analogy with the family situation, then theism is very likely to encourage parochialism. As the familiar Christian saying goes, charity begins at home, and this saying has been honored in actual practice; for though deeply religious persons in the traditional theistic sense have often engaged in private charity and have often acted in a spirit of noble self-sacrifice, the impetus for large-scale social reform has usually come from dominantly secular groups, such as the utilitarians, the Marxists, and the pragmatists. It is only recently, with the secularization of the churches themselves and under the influence of these secular movements, that any sizable number of religious groups have joined in, and then only half-heartedly. The program and the fate of the so-called Social Gospel movement is worth pondering in this connection. Moreover, it is not without significance that Stoicism, with its emphasis upon duty, rather than Christianity, with its emphasis upon love, was the movement that first introduced cosmopolitan ideas to the Western world. If the argument in Chapter VI is correct, it is the circumstances giving rise to the sense of duty rather than those giving rise to the spirit of benevolence that most firmly and surely foster the sense of a human community.

My conclusion is that attempts to demonstrate the beneficial moral consequences of theistic belief fail. But this does not exhaust the case against theism. Theism not only fails to encourage the practice of morality but actually inhibits it.

1. At best, arguments for the existence of a personal deity and of a system of rewards and punishments after death are weak. It is, therefore, almost inevitable that theists would tend to regard rationality with mistrust, and, as a matter of historical fact, most of them have and still do. Now, if the arguments in preceding chapters are correct, this mistrust of reason cannot but inhibit the development of strong moral character. Especially to be regretted is the common theistic espousal of that doctrine according to which virtue attaches to faith, where faith is understood as belief in dogmas for which no rational evidence is available. Faith so understood is closely allied with fanaticism.

2. Since theism envisages God as a father and depends very largely for its appeal upon attitudes formed in early childhood, it has a strong tendency to blow up the childish virtues of obedience and humility out of all due proportion. It encourages what Kant and Piaget call heteronomous, as opposed to autonomous, ethics, undermining the individual's sense of independence, self-reliance, and simple human dignity. To use the stronger language of Nietzsche, it encourages the adoption of a morality fit only for slaves.

3. To the extent that theism succeeds in persuading men of

personal immortality, it tends to reduce their sense of concern for social betterment in this world. From the standpoint of eternity, the individual's seventy-odd years on this planet and even the total history of mankind pale into insignificance. It might be countered here that by investing individual human beings with a significance they would not otherwise have, the belief in immortality has not the effect I just suggested but rather its opposite. Were we not to believe in individual immortality, we would have little reason to believe in the sacredness and worth of individual human beings. The truth or falsity of this rejoinder is a question I shall not try to decide, for even if it were true that our concern for human beings would be enhanced if we regarded them as immortal souls, it would remain the case that our enhanced concern would be not with their earthly well-being, but with the fate of their immortal souls.

RELIGIOUS OPTIMISM

Although theism constitutes the core of the Western religious tradition, there are two other very powerful Western religious outlooks that call for discussion. To these outlooks I shall give the names "religious optimism" and "religious pessimism." My justification for treating them separately from theism is that they have many nontheistic versions and raise problems of an altogether different kind from those associated with theism. For many theists, however, religious optimism or religious pessimism is an integral part of their outlook.

By religious optimism I mean to denote substantially the type of religious outlook that William James referred to as "healthy-mindedness" and that Kierkegaard referred to under the name of "religiosity A." Its essential tenet is that the totality of what exists constitutes a harmoniously integrated whole of which individual human beings are but parts and that this harmoniously integrated whole is a metaphysical or religious good. Everything that happens, since it is but a part of this larger whole, must also be good.

The metaphysical tradition in which this view was developed reaches back at least as far as the Stoics. Christian theologians often found religious optimism necessary as a means of reconciling the benevolence and justice of God with his omnipotence. It has found its most consistent development in Spinoza, Leibniz, and Bradley, and its most grotesque recent expressions at the hands of Mary Baker Eddy and Norman Vincent Peale.

A number of Christian mystics, Spinoza, and many of the more pantheistic nature-worshipers of nineteenth-century romanticism poetized religious optimism and gave it a romantic twist. The Calvinists and the Puritans, on the other hand, gave it a moralistic twist. In the romantic version, being is viewed aesthetically or quasi-tragically and is regarded as a thing of beauty. Evil and suffering are said to have no positive reality. We can speak of evil and suffering only because we have not attained a satisfactory vision of the whole. Religious experience for those who hold to this romanticized version of religious optimism reduces to a mystic experience of participation in God or Nature during which finitude is overcome and we see the totality of what exists *sub specie aeternitatis,* under the aspect of eternity. Evil and suffering are merely the darker shades serving to set in relief the brighter shades of the picture, which properly viewed is unqualifiedly good. In the moralistic version of religious optimism being is viewed ethically and is regarded as a realm of justice. The existence and positive reality of evil and suffering are not denied, but suffering is regarded as the just desert of the sinful. Religious experience for the ethical optimists consists almost entirely in a sense of guilt or of self-righteousness and a dogged effort to observe the divine commandments.

Of course, the romanticized and the moralistic versions of religious optimism have usually been combined in its major historical representatives, notably St. Augustine and Leibniz. The two doctrines are not, however, easily reconciled, and one or the other tends to predominate. One cannot logically assert the legitimacy of adopting a higher perspective from which good and evil may be said to be illusory while at the same time arguing that moral evil is a positive reality demanding real suffering as punishment.

Of contemporary religious movements neo-Thomism and Protestant liberalism are the most heavily impregnated with religious optimism. For neo-Thomists and Protestant liberals alike, man is essentially a created being whose status is determined by divine ordinance. God created the world and found it *good.* He placed man *within* the world, gave him dominion over the lower animals, and provided him with an abundance of good things—more than enough for his well-being and comfort. The sole condition of God's bounty is that man observe God's natural and moral laws. By the right use of his reason, man may know these laws; and by the right use of his free will, he may conform to them in his behavior. The suffering of an individual must, therefore, be interpreted as a just punishment for sinful disobedience—moralistic optimism. The harshness of this doctrine is, however, somewhat dispelled by combining it with the view that suffering is a necessary feature of the divine economy for which the individual will be abundantly compensated in an afterlife. From the larger perspective the individual's sufferings may, therefore, be regarded as a necessary but transitory phase in the divine plan—romantic optimism.

The Protestant liberals tend to ignore or summarily dismiss the dogmas of the fall, of divine grace, and of eternal torments in hell. The neo-Thomists find a place for these doctrines, but as a rule they are kept comfortably in the background. The neo-Thomists are emphatic in asserting that the fall did not affect man's essential nature, and although respect for tradition often obliges them to say that grace is both a necessary and a sufficient condition of salvation, they tend to forget that they have said this and inconsistently stress the role of rational and voluntary adherence to moral law.

There are a number of reasons why religious optimism is unsatisfactory:

1. On the score of rationality it is only a few degrees superior to theism. It is very difficult to believe that we could meaningfully

qualify the whole of what exists as either good or bad. If we use a term such as "good" to describe the whole of things, we are using "good" in a sense for which no clear meaning bearing any connection with its meaning in ordinary discourse has ever been specified. Moreover, we are not capable of viewing the totality of what exists *sub specie aeternitatis,* so that even if we could meaningfully qualify the whole of things as good we should still never be in a position to verify the contention that it is good.

2. Although religious optimism appears at first sight to be a healthy-minded philosophy with great consolatory power, the appearances are deceptive. If we accept religious optimism in its aesthetic version, we simply license ourselves to wallow in sentimentality. If we accept it in its moralistic version, we tend to oscillate between an attitude of self-righteousness when life is treating us well and an attitude of guilty self-abasement when life is treating us ill. There is nothing healthy-minded about any of these attitudes.

To deny that life is tragic is, indeed, one way of reconciling oneself to tragedy, and to deny that injustice exists is, indeed, one way of restoring faith in the moral order. But few who have had a true taste of suffering or who have been victims of serious injustice are able sincerely to accept the doctrine. Desperation may drive a man to embrace religious optimism, as it did Spinoza,[2] but most of the persons who profess it are comfortably entrenched in the bourgeois routine of existence, and it is unlikely that their religious professions are more than conventional. Moreover, most versions of religious optimism are avowedly based upon the

[2] Spinoza tells us how he was led to religious optimism in the following famous passage:

> I thus perceived that I was in a state of great peril, and I compelled myself to seek with all my strength for a remedy, however uncertain it might be; as a sick man struggling with a deadly disease, when he sees that death will surely be upon him unless a remedy be found, is compelled to seek such a remedy with all his strength, inasmuch as his whole hope lies therein. [Baruch Spinoza, "On the Improvement of the Understanding," trans. Elwes and Bohn, in *Spinoza,* ed. John Wild (New York: Charles Scribner's Sons, 1930), p. 3.]

pessimistic assumption that any attempt substantially to satisfy the plurality of our particular desires is doomed to fail. Our particular desires, Spinoza pointed out, are desires of the perishable; and love of the perishable produces quarrels, sadness, envy, fear, and hatred. However, the assumption that happiness cannot be achieved through a rational pursuit of worldly goals is refuted daily; and although love of the perishable often produces quarrels, sadness, envy, fear, and hatred, it also produces the most sublime, poignant, and richly satisfying experiences that most of us are capable of knowing. The delights of music, poetry, theater, art, and literature; the excitement of foreign travel; the joys of creativity; humor; the innocent pleasures of the senses; the love of friend for friend, of man and woman, of parents for their children —are these things less satisfying, less easily attainable, more costly, or less lasting than a vision of life *sub specie aeternitatis?*

3. Religious optimism cannot but tend to deprive us of moral energy. Although James's good sense completely deserted him when he gave to religious optimism the name of healthy-mindedness, he was perfectly right in calling it a moral holiday. It is as if religious optimism were designed to still our protest against social injustice and to preserve the *status quo.* As St. Paul said in a text that Luther found of use against the oppressed German peasants: "Let every soul be subject unto the higher powers. For there is no power but of God; the powers that be are ordained of God. Whosoever therefore resisteth the power, resisteth the ordinance of God; and they that resist shall receive unto themselves damnation."[3] Echoes of this view persist: "If," says one contemporary Christian conservative thinker, "our world is ordered in accordance with a Divine idea, we ought to be cautious in our tinkering with the structure of society; for though it may be God's will that we serve as his instruments of alteration, we need first to satisfy our consciences on this point."[4]

[3] Romans, 13:1–2.

[4] Russell Kirk, *The Conservative Mind* (Chicago: Henry Regnery Co., 1953), p. 30.

RELIGIOUS PESSIMISM

By "religious pessimism" I mean to denote roughly the kind of religious philosophy that Kierkegaard labeled "religiosity B" and which James contrasted with healthy-mindedness. Religious pessimism, although popular on the European continent, has only begun to make itself felt as an important social force in America. In essence, religious pessimism consists of the view that an acute and anguished awareness of evil and suffering, together with an uncompromising recognition of our finitude and thus of the impossibility of contemplating or experiencing being *sub specie aeternitatis,* is itself the chief value of life. We are so constituted that we cannot abandon the search for the fullness and perfection of being that would be ours only if we attained such a vision of life, but the very nature of our being is such that we cannot hope to attain it. It is as if man were thrown into the world and left there—alone, sick, and afraid. It is as if God had forsaken him, as he did Christ on the cross, but only after having taught him to be unhappy with anything less than beatitude. Such is our condition. Anguish is an inescapable fact of life; Kierkegaard called it "the sickness unto death." But within this very anguish and despair that constitutes our being, we find the glory and the beauty of life. To flee from it or to deny it is simply to transform it into a banal anxiety or a prosaic fear. In the words of Unamuno: ". . . the remedy is to consider our moral destiny without flinching, to fasten our gaze upon the gaze of the Sphinx, for it is thus that the malevolence of its spell is discharmed."[5] We must not attempt to escape from suffering but rather to convert it into a religious joy. The last line of Unamuno's *Tragic Sense of Life* summarizes this position very well: "And may God deny you peace but give you glory."

Religious pessimism has deep roots not only in historical

[5] Miguel de Unamuno, *The Tragic Sense of Life,* trans. Flitch (New York: Dover Publications, Inc., 1954), p. 9.

Christianity but also in the pre-Christian oriental mystery religions. It has, however, been most fully developed by the existentialists—atheistic existentialists like Nietzsche, Heidegger, Sartre, and Camus no less than theistic existentialists like Kierkegaard, Unamuno, Buber, Berdyaev, Chestov, Landsberg, and Marcel. It has also been reflected in neo-orthodox thinkers such as Barth, Niebuhr, and to a lesser extent Tillich.

For the most part I shall draw illustrations from the Christian existentialists, but it is important to realize that religious pessimism need not be theistic. Atheistic existentialism, it has been said, is essentially "a discourse on the absence of God."[6] Sartre is fond of quoting the remark of Nietzsche that he and other contemporary existentialists have now made famous: "God is dead." Sartre's complaint, like Nietzsche's, is that people try to go on living as lightheartedly as though he were still alive. If God is dead, says Sartre, man must try to take his place. In fact, Sartre has defined man as the being who can never be God but who can never stop wanting to be God. Heidegger tells us that man's hopeless search for the fullness of being that the Christians believe God to possess and that the very nature of man's being prevents him from ever attaining is, like original sin, a doom upon us all. We live authentically only when we think of death and thereby acquire an acute consciousness of the essential vanity of worldly projects. The anguish of death is a revelation of the essence of human existence, and the essence of human existence is expressed in his famous slogan "being for death" (*Sein zum Tode*). For Sartre and Camus life is a perpetual and inevitable series of failures; the only ultimate value, the only thing that makes life really noble and worthwhile, is the willingness to look this fact in the face and to go right on failing. Both of these authors insist that it is only after having discovered the essential absurdity of human existence that we can live with verve and a keen sense of our human responsibilities. It is only when we realize the vanity

[6] The phrase is that of E. Levinas, quoted in A. de Waehlens, *La Philosophie de Martin Heidegger* (Louvain: Éditions de l'Institut Superieur de Philosophie, 1948), p. 164.

of our endeavors that they become invested with meaning. The myth of Sisyphus, which Camus took as the title of his famous wartime book, was chosen to symbolize the human condition; and the myth of Prometheus, to symbolize the proper ethical attitude.

Like religious optimism, religious pessimism has both an ethical and a romantic version. Ethical versions of religious pessimism are not uncommon, and Paul would have to call most existentialists to order, as he did the Romans, for "sinning the more that grace may abound."[7] Kierkegaard said that the "idea, the view of life, of knowing all evil, which a gnostic sect made its own, is profound. . . . Yes, I believe that I would give myself to Satan so that he might show me every abomination, every sin in its most frightful form. . . ."[8] Consider also the fascination and the indulgence of Sartre for self-styled "black saints" like Jean Genet. It is, however, the romantic version that predominates. Again, to quote Kierkegaard, "the decisive mark of Christian suffering is that it is voluntary."[9] Joy, said Nietzsche, is deeper than suffering, but anguish and suffering are our only access to this deeper joy.

The Christian existentialist and the Protestant neo-orthodox, unlike the Protestant liberal and the neo-Thomist, place the dogma of the fall and of divine grace in the center of their philosophy and accept the logical consequences—more properly, the paradoxes to which these doctrines inevitably lead. They are united in the conviction that man's place is not within nature, and all, without exception, insist that God's laws are unknowable by natural reason and that man's natural will is impotent. The natural man is a fallen man whose nature has been radically altered by his fall. The ideal of a City of God on earth, that is to say, the ideal of a reasonably well-adjusted, smoothly operating social organism is condemned as an unrealizable dream. Berdyaev is an exception here. Unlike most existentialists, he claims that this utopian dream of complete social and natural well-being is

[7] Romans, 6:1.

[8] Sören Kierkegaard, *Journals,* trans. and ed. Alender Dru (London: Oxford University Press, 1938), p. 41 (first pub. abt. 1900).

[9] Kierkegaard, *Training in Christianity,* trans. Lowrie (London: Oxford University Press, 1941), p. 111 (first pub. 1850).

realizable, but he hastens to add that its realization is what is most to be feared. The dream is really a nightmare.[10] Aldous Huxley even quotes him to this effect on the frontispiece to *Brave New World,* and, of course, if the kind of world Huxley there depicted is what the existentialists mean by the utopian dream of natural well-being I can agree that it is nightmarish. The point, however, is this. For the existentialists, man is so constituted by his nature that happiness necessarily implies a loss of other and greater positive values.

For the existentialists and the neo-orthodox, man's status is that of an exile—not only from the Kingdom of God but also from the Kingdom of Nature. When the existentialists talk about the human condition, it is precisely this status as a forlorn and suffering exile that they have in mind. "What other feelings," asks Chestov, "can one entertain for the natural order and humanitarian sentiments than unqualified hate? Spencer taught adaptation—the moralists, resignation. But this instruction is valuable only if one supposes that adaptation is still possible or that resignation can give us a certain relief. . . ."[11] In a text that beautifully complements that of Chestov, Berdyaev writes:

> The ethics of the ancients, especially the classical ethics of Aristotle, considered man a being who seeks happiness, good and harmony, and who is capable of achieving this goal. Such is also the point of St. Thomas Aquinas and of the official Catholic theology. But in fact Christianity has shaken this view. Kant, Schopenhauer, Nietzsche and Dostoievsky are important witnesses to the fact. . . . Not the worst but the best of mankind suffer the most. The intensity with which suffering is felt may be considered an index of a man's depth. The more the intellect is developed and the soul refined . . . the more sensitive does one become to pain, not only the pains of the soul but physical pains as well. . . . But for pain and suffering the animal in man would be victorious.[12]

[10] Nicolas Berdyaev, *Un Nouveau Moyen-age* (Paris: Librairie Plon, 1927), pp. 262–63.

[11] Leon Chestov, *La Philosophie de la tragédie,* trans. Schloezer (Paris: J. Schiffrin, 1926), p. 188.

[12] Nicolas Berdyaev, *Dialectique existentielle du divin et de l'humain* (Paris: J. B. Janin, 1947), pp. 96–97.

The religious pessimists view life as the lonely sojourn of an exile without guide or compass, whose misery is part of his glory and whose sinfulness is a part of his being. Spiritual worth consists not of the strained quest after moral perfection but of a free acceptance of the human condition. The self-righteousness of the well-adjusted and the pretended certainty of the believer are but the disguised pride of original sinners. If they but knew their true status, self-righteousness would give way to an anguished awareness of finitude, and certainty would give way to tortured faith. The harmonious adjustment of man to man and of man to nature with its accompanying peace of mind, which the Protestant liberal and neo-Thomist tend to regard as a sign of healthy adjustment to the divine order, are for the existentialists obstacles to the truly religious life. Doubt, suffering, anguish, and passion become positive values rather than indexes of maladjustment. The natural light of reason and voluntary self-control are deprecated.

Religious pessimism is in some respects an improvement over religious optimism. There are countless persons whose chances for natural happiness are practically nil, and there are times when life is too much for all of us. The religious pessimists have rendered an invaluable service in attacking the superficial optimism that led to the neglect of such obvious cases and in putting the question of evil and suffering anew, at a profounder level. They also deserve credit for having seen that when the resources of intelligence and voluntary effort have been exhausted, any attempt to relieve suffering by a stubborn and hopeless effort at adaptation will succeed only in changing the felt quality of experience into something mean, petty, and crabbed, while any attempt to relieve suffering by mystic identification with God or Nature simply reduces tragedy to bathos.

None the less religious pessimism is also unsatisfactory.

1. It presupposes a needlessly paradoxical theory of human nature. On the one hand, the religious pessimists claim that man is somehow destined for the tragic but sublime and glorious experience of joy in suffering and that by his very nature he would prefer this to natural well-being. On the other hand, they present joy in suffering as a desperate remedy to a desperate situation, a

leap in the dark away from an intolerable world. But they cannot have it both ways. Either man is destined for glory, or he is not. Either a life with occasional experiences of the kind existentialists describe and much natural suffering or moral evil is preferable to a life of natural well-being without evil and glory, or else it is not. No matter how strongly the religious pessimist insists upon the aesthetic value of the experience of anguish, he admits either that the dominant affective component is one of pain or that its price is great misery, from which it is reasonable to conclude that the attempt to escape the natural and social dimensions of life is at least as self-defeating as the attempt to escape anguish and suffering. Furthermore, in the absence of more positive considerations pointing in the other direction, the temporal priority of natural drives is presumptive evidence of their primacy in the scale of values.

2. For deeply religious persons who have been victims of injustice or forced to undergo extreme suffering, religious pessimism does have greater consolatory power than religious optimism; but consolation of this kind is purchased at a heavy cost, namely, the deliberate pursuit of further suffering for which one may, in turn, be consoled. Forgetting that the decisive mark of Christian suffering is that it is voluntary, Kierkegaard tells us that naturally religious men are persons whom society has cut off and made to suffer, as he was cut off and made to suffer. Having thus been turned to God, however, he was made into a prophet. "What our age needs," he writes, "is education. And so this is what happened: God chose a man who also needed to be educated, and educated him *privatissime* so that he might be able to teach others from his own experience."[13] We learn elsewhere that the chosen one was Kierkegaard himself. Now, I do not understand why God should choose those who suffer as his saints and prophets, nor do I understand why he would make his saints and prophets suffer. The claim that suffering is a religious value has never, as far as I know, been backed up by reasoned argument, and it is most naturally explicable as a compensatory psychological device. Given this assumption, however, it is not only rea-

[13] Kierkegaard, *Journals*, p. 199.

sonable that a man should voluntarily pursue suffering, but it is inevitable that his sufferings should occasion a particularly vicious form of spiritual pride.

3. This brings me to a third objection. Religious pessimism tends just as naturally as religious optimism to sap the sources of moral energy. If natural well-being is an unattainable ideal and if its effect is to deprive us of superior values, there is no satisfactory justification for pursuing it. Attempted justification will be pitifully lame. Consider the following text from Paul-Louis Landsberg:

> If suffering is sacred and if the meaning of life lies therein, why have we the right to fight against it? . . . I do, indeed, believe that we have the right to struggle against the miseries of human existence. The opposite thesis would obviously lead to absurd ethical conclusions: the immorality of medical practice, for example. But neither the importance of this fight nor the possibilities of success should be overestimated. It is natural and highly praiseworthy for us to struggle against sickness, cruelty, poverty, etc. . . . But the truth is that in the last analysis history reveals no progress in the direction of human happiness. The direction of historical development is rather in the opposite direction. Available evidence indicates that the so-called primitive peoples are far happier than others. The mistake lies not in the struggle against suffering but in the illusion that we are able to abolish it. The most efficacious form of the fight against suffering is work, a method imposed upon man both as a punishment and as a remedy.[14]

Kierkegaard was more consistent in admitting that Abraham the murderer cannot be regarded as Abraham the knight of faith without paradox. Christianity, he said, is "treason against humanity."[15] And so was Sir Leonard Woolf when he wrote: "Christianity envisages a framework for human society in which earthly miseries have a recognized, permanent, and honorable place. . . . It is impious to repine against them."[16]

14 Paul-Louis Landsberg, *Problème moral du suicide* (Paris: Éditions du Seuil, 1951), p. 150.

15 Kierkegaard, *For Self-Examination,* trans. Lowrie (London: Oxford University Press, 1941), p. 155.

16 Sir Leonard Woolf, *After the Deluge* (New York: Harcourt, Brace & World, Inc., 1931), p. 219.

RELIGIOUS NATURALISM

To sum up the argument so far, theism, religious optimism, and religious pessimism are each deficient on three counts. First, all of these religious outlooks involve nonrational beliefs. Whatever the merits of this or that argument in support of one or another tenet of theism, the ensemble of theistic beliefs cannot be rationally defended. Neither can the belief that the totality of things is good, or the belief that natural well-being is not a genuine good. Second, no one of these religious philosophies has great consolatory power. In theism the fear of eternal damnation cancels out the hope of an eternal reward. Religious optimism is so patently absurd that few persons who really need consolation can sustain belief in it. And religious pessimism provides consolation only at a cost that no rational man would wish to pay. Third, each of these religious outlooks has a strong tendency to undermine our sense of moral responsibility and little if any tendency to inspire zeal for social reform. Theism tends to emphasize private charity to the detriment of effective social action. Religious optimism blinds us to the very existence of suffering and injustice. Religious pessimism, by elevating suffering to a status of supreme value, weakens our concern to diminish it.

Religious naturalism suffers from none of these weaknesses. (1) First and foremost, the religious naturalist believes that man is a rational animal who cannot live by rationally unfounded dogmas without paying a greater price than any temporary benefits such belief may bring are worth. Accordingly, he recognizes that man is the source of his own values and that these values must be realized largely through his own rational and voluntary efforts. He recognizes that man does want natural well-being and that natural well-being is a good. Practically all human desires are oriented toward that end, and we do not seek joy in suffering or mystic identification with God or nature as long as natural well-being is attainable. Nor do we, as long as we are happy, suffer unduly from the fear of death. (2) The naturalist regards suffering as a tragic but more or less permanent fact of human existence that can be neither ignored nor transmuted. He is neither ashamed of suffering nor disposed to seek it out. When he must suffer, he will try to suffer with dignity; and when he sees others suffer he will sympathize whole-heartedly, knowing that affection and the sense of human solidarity are and always have been the most important source of comfort in times of distress. (3) The naturalist believes that the only really substantial remedy for human ills is social improvement. He will not therefore belittle the intelligent efforts at social reform and individual self-control necessary to its achievement. "One of the few experiments in the attachment of emotion to ends that mankind has not tried," writes John Dewey, "is that of devotion, so intense as to be religious, to intelligence as a force in social action."[17] The religious naturalist is dedicated to that experiment.

Within religious naturalism so defined there are two wings: a left and a right. The classic statement of left-wing naturalism is that of Bertrand Russell in his famous essay "A Free Man's Worship," written in 1902:

> Such, in outline, but even more purposeless, more void of meaning, is the world which Science presents for our belief. Amid such a world, if anywhere, our ideals henceforward must find a home. That man is the product of causes which had no prevision of the end they were achieving; that his origin, his growth, his hopes and fears, his loves and his beliefs, are but the outcome of accidental collocations of atoms; that no fire, no heroism, no intensity of thought and feeling, can preserve an individual life beyond the grave; that all the labours of the ages, all the devotion, all the inspirations, all the noonday brightness of human genius, are destined to extinction in the vast death of the solar system, and that the whole temple of Man's achievement must inevitably be buried beneath the debris of a universe in ruins—all these things, if not quite beyond dispute, are yet so nearly certain, that no philosophy which rejects them can hope to stand. Only within the scaffolding of these truths, only on the firm foundation of unyielding despair, can the soul's habitation henceforth be safely built.

[17] John Dewey, *A Common Faith* (New Haven: Yale University Press, 1934), p. 79.

. . .

> Brief and powerless is Man's life; on him and all his race the slow, sure doom falls pitiless and dark. Blind to good and evil, reckless of destruction, omnipotent matter rolls on its relentless way; for Man, condemned today to lose his dearest, tomorrow himself to pass through the gate of darkness, it remains only to cherish, ere yet the blow falls, the lofty thoughts that ennoble his little day; disdaining the coward terrors of the slave of Fate, to worship at the shrine that his own hands have built; undismayed by the empire of chance, to preserve a mind free from the wanton tyranny that rules his outward life; proudly defiant of the irresistible forces that tolerate, for a moment, his knowledge and his condemnation, to sustain alone, a weary but unyielding Atlas, the world that his own ideals have fashioned despite the trampling march of unconscious power.[18]

Right-wing naturalism is best represented by John Dewey in *A Common Faith.* There, as elsewhere, he argued that the most worthy of human ideals is the harmonious adjustment of man to nature and of man to man, that intelligence is the most satisfactory means to the attainment of this goal, and that the matter-of-fact assumption of an active and responsible role in our natural and social environment is the best solution to our personal ills.

Russellian naturalism, it will readily be seen, veers toward religious pessimism, particularly the religious pessimism of the atheistic existentialists. Deweyan naturalism, on the other hand, veers toward religious optimism. Russell emphasizes unyielding pride and Promethean defiance. Dewey emphasizes a sense of continuity with nature. Moreover, each has attacked the other. Russell complains that Dewey's philosophy reflects a shallow optimism, while Dewey no doubt had Russell in mind when he wrote the following passage:

> Militant atheism is also affected by lack of natural piety. The ties binding man to nature that poets have always celebrated are passed over lightly. The attitude taken is often that of man living in an indifferent and hostile world and issuing blasts of defiance. A religious attitude, however, needs the sense of connection of man, in

[18] Bertrand Russell, *Mysticism and Logic* (London: George Allen & Unwin, Ltd., 1917), pp. 47, 56–57.

the way of both dependence and support, with the enveloping world that the imagination feels is a universe.[19]

One must not, however, identify right-wing naturalism with religious optimism. The religious optimist deifies nature per se. Dewey searches out the divine in the projection of human ideals and the imaginative reconstruction of nature by human intelligence. The religious optimist, moreover, will have us detach ourselves from wordly concerns. Dewey urges us to fulfill ourselves in and through the world.

Neither ought one to identify left-wing naturalism with atheistic religious pessimism. For the religious pessimist of the atheistic variety, human worth and dignity consist almost exclusively of an attitude of revolt and defiance. For Russell, revolt and defiance, though proper and worthy human attitudes under trying circumstances, are neither the only nor the chief of human values. For Russell, man is essentially an intelligent animal with a superior cultural endowment who seeks happiness and harmony and who under favorable conditions is capable of achieving that goal.

Finally, one ought not to exaggerate the differences between right-wing and left-wing religious naturalism. Dewey certainly agrees with Russell that we have not the slightest reason to suppose the existence of an intelligent nonhuman agency from which man may expect support in the achievement of his deepest aspirations. And Russell will certainly grant to Dewey that within limits man can and does utilize the forces of nature to sustain and promote human well-being. Moreover, both men agree that in the last analysis it is not a specific vision of man's place in nature but rather the exercise of reason and the practice of human sympathy in the finite world of practical affairs that constitute human worth. Their differences have little to do either with their basic convictions as to the nature of the universe or their fundamental value orientation. The relevant difference turns on the moral and consolatory value of what are essentially emotive-pictorial beliefs. And even on this point their differences are less profound than might be thought, since both men would probably agree that a

19 Dewey, *op. cit.*, p. 53.

decision with respect to the appropriateness of permitting or cultivating specific emotive-pictorial beliefs depends in large part on individual temperament and particular circumstances. When and to the extent that nature proves amenable to the designs of human intention, it is almost inevitable and quite proper that we permit ourselves to represent it symbolically as a friendly and co-operative force. When, however, and to the extent that the battle of man and nature becomes too unequal, the darker vision of the universe is not unnatural or unworthy, since it will often lead to a renewed dedication to the cause of human welfare.

There is, then, but one further point that I wish to raise. Naturalism, it is often said, however adequate it may be theoretically, cannot qualify as a religion because it cannot appeal to the deeper reaches of the human personality. It is without poetry and without affective appeal. Now, to be sure, naturalism has not been codified in dogma; it has no priests, no rituals, and no cathedrals. But it is not without affective appeal, and it is not without myths and symbols. The fact is that it has all the myths and symbols that could possibly be desired: practically the whole of the world's great literature. The left-wing naturalist can claim not only Greek tragedy and Shakespeare, which obviously come to mind, but also the Old Testament. In fact, he has a far better claim on the Old Testament than the theist, the religious optimist, or the religious pessimist. Whatever else Yahweh may have done, he did not invite his creatures to share in his divinity, nor did he reward them for voluntary suffering. He was a jealous and a capricious God whom no man could approach and who, if he bothered to reward his servants at all, did so not with ecstasy, suffering, or immortal bliss, but with sons and cows. Interpreted metaphorically, the God of the Old Testament is a personification of the indifferent forces of nature from which by enterprise and cunning man can wrest an occasional favor. The right-wing naturalist, on the other hand, can claim every scrap of literature that has ever sung praise to human achievement and that has recognized that the world man inhabits is the supreme accomplishment of the imaginative powers of a race that, to paraphrase Faulkner's famous words, may not only endure but prevail.

INDEX